Call to Healing

A Way of Life in the Church

Rev. Chuck Gallagher, S.J.

Nihil Obstat Rev. Peter Chirico, S.S. STD
              Archdiocesan Censor

Imprimatur ✠ Raymond G. Hunthausen D.D.
              Archbishop of Seattle
              September 16, 1982

The *nihil obstat* and *imprimatur* are official declarations that a book or pamphlet is free of doctrinal or moral error. No implication is contained therein that those who have granted the nihil obstat or imprimatur agree with the contents, opinions, or statements expressed.

Copyright © 1982 by William H. Sadlier, Inc. All rights reserved. This book, or any part thereof, may not be reproduced in any form, or by any means, including electronic, photographic, or mechanical, or by any sound recording system, or by any device for storage and retrieval of information, without the written permission of the publisher. Printed in the United States of America.

Published by William H. Sadlier, Inc.
11 Park Place
New York, New York 10007

ISBN: 0-8215-9873-2
123456789/98765432

Library of Congress Number: 82-061454

Table of Contents

	Foreword	v
1	Healing in the Church	7
2	Healing: A Charism of the Church	18
3	Healing Takes Time	25
4	The Healing Ceremony: General Session	41
5	Core Groups and Sub-Groups	62
6	Sub-Group I: Virtues Needed for Healing	71
7	Sub-Group II: Identifying My Hurts and Where I Need Healing	90
8	Sub-Group III: The Healing Proper	106
9	Witness to the Healing: Thanksgiving	112

Foreword

Jesus came to save persons, not just souls. He came to bring persons closer to the Father and to one another in every aspect of their beings. That is why he did more than forgive sins. He cast out devils, he cured the sick, he raised the dead, he instructed the ignorant, and he brought the separated together. In short, he came to heal us in all that we are and in all our relationships.

In this book Father Gallagher takes up the global healing ministry of the Church. He recognizes that certain aspects of healing are carried out by doctors, counselors, and problem solvers. Yet he sees the Church as a whole as being involved in the deeper and more ultimate healing that all persons need. In a practical manner he sets forth a way in which the Church can organize itself as a healing community. He shows that the work of healing, while it begins with corporate prayer, sacrifice, concern for others, and openness to the Father, is ultimately a sacramental healing.

I hope that many Christians will be helped by this book to appreciate their dignity as members of a healing community. May these pages inspire them to enter into the Church's healing ministry and instruct them to participate in that call in a manner that is loyal to our Tradition.

September 1, 1982   Raymond G. Hunthausen
                           Archbishop of Seattle

Special thanks to Jack and Cathy Colligan

for their very generous interest
and work on the manuscript

1 HEALING HURTS IN THE CHURCH

All of us, at least at one time or another, experience hurts. By hurts we mean those resulting from personal experiences that we have had in dealing with specific other people. Our hurts cause us to keep our distance from those persons—to build a wall between us. That produces a layer of loneliness, alienation, anomie within us. When the intensity or depth of the hurts is great enough we develop an anger within us. At first, we become defensive and then protective. Sometimes we are very hostile and looking for people to offend us. We become very critical and judgmental. We are constantly picking at people and looking to find in them the flaws we dislike. We become unpleasant people to be with and we surround ourselves with people who fuel our anger. We become crusaders for our own rights. Or we may choose to wear the martyr's crown and fall into a pattern of self-pity.

We turn inward and we even avoid all other people. Life each day becomes boring and distasteful. We become depressed and confined, as though caught in a bottle with a tight cork. If only we could be relieved, let the pressure off, be unburdened, be reconciled with others. Wouldn't it be great relief if we could purge our hurts even in those situations where the "other party" cannot easily be reconciled with us? (Consider the case of someone who stubbornly refuses to reconcile or may be far away or dead or so threatening that we dare not approach him or her directly.)

Healing in the Body of Christ

There is a way. And it is ours for the asking through the source of all healing—the Body of Christ. Each baptized person is a member of this Body and each has been commissioned to heal, to reconcile the hurts in his brothers and sisters. We have long overlooked this special mission of our local church, our parish. We believe, however, that if we return to this healing work in our parish the joy of Jesus will become alive in our hearts and each one of us will live a more exciting, hope-filled, and enriched life.

It hardly seems necessary to establish the fact that hurts are prevalent throughout the Church today. We simply have to do something about them. The basic problems facing the Church are not theological or ethical but personal. Hurts cause far more damage to the believability of the Body of Christ than we can ever imagine. We need to come to grips with these hurts in a broad-scale way in the Church, not just handling them piece-meal, on a one-on-one or emergency out-patient basis. In one way or other, almost everybody in the Church carries deep hurts, specifically in terms of being Church, as well as the normal personal hurts all of us experience. Until we face these hurts and do something to create an environment and atmosphere of healing on a broad scale, we are going to be struggling as a Church. Futhermore, this healing has to take place on the grass-roots level, that is, in the parish.

We have not yet truly come to grips with the importance of healing in the Church. What healing is taking place tends to be peripheral and separated from a specific missioning of the Church. It is done by different individuals and different groups, some sounder than others but all independent. If a parish is to be truly caring and concerned about the parishioners, then healing has to be one of the major outreaches of each diocese and each parish. Instead of being an exception and the object of a special activity outside the parish, healing should be a *normal* part of parish life. We would like to see it as available to parishioners as the Eucharist and the sacrament of Reconciliation. The reason for this view is not far to seek, when we consider the damaged relationships all around us in the Church and recall the means Jesus gave us for healing one another in His name.

It follows then that the pastor must come to see healing as part of his normal role. He can no longer afford to leave this ministry to others while he concentrates his efforts elsewhere. His people need to see in him the source of their reconciliation and unity.

Damaged Relationships

Here are some examples of damaged family relationships that we as parish leaders should look into to see if we cannot offer a healing for them. They are typical examples; not extreme cases. Our tendency, when we think of hurts, is to think of dramatic extraordinary ones. But we have to recognize that it is more commonly the dull, aching sobs that interfere with relationships and damage the Body of Christ. A healing experience established within the parish from the graces that have been given to us in our sacrament of healing would be a real gift to people in these circumstances.

• *Those who are having difficulties with parenting.* Of course, there will be those who are in extreme cases: a child who has run away from home, or parents and children waging constant cold wars or having a lot of arguments. Yet, we should not exclude the more normal type of situations, for everybody has difficulty with parenting at every age of parenting. Parenting problems may arise when the children are very little or when they have grown up a little bit, or especially in teenage and young adult years. But there may also be the trouble in parenting of adult children who have married and have children of their own.

We want to concentrate on offering a healing for the sense of ingratitude that many parents experience from their children, whether it is intended or not. For example:

a. the feeling of hopelessness—that the children are out of control as they get older, and that as parents they have not real influence over their children's lives;
b. the put-down that many parents experience from their children also see them as being "out of it;"
c. the pain that parents are experiencing because of children who have left the Church or who are not terribly interested in it;
d. the pain of parents who have been accused of playing favorites with the children, or the pain of parents whose children are in a bad marriage, or who have a pregnant, unmarried daughter. (One of the dangers we have to avoid here is not just to support the girl's mother. Very frequently the man suffers even more excruci-

ating agony when his daughter gets pregnant. Unless we surface that fact and talk openly about it, our men are not going to face it.)
e. the pain parents experience with regard to changes in religious education—most especially with how children are prepared for the sacraments.

In all of these things, we are not normally talking about a single, isolated event, but about patterns of behavior.

● *The pains of children from parents, i.e., adults as well as the young.* We have to recognize that parent-child problems are not a one-way street. Many children are badly hurt because they believe their parents do not understand them, are too authoritarian, are not around enough, or run the house as the family belongs to the parents alone and not to the children as well. The guilt that the children feel is a result of believing they have been manipulated.

● *Those whose children are leaving or have left the house.*

● *The time of adolescence, for both the parent and the child.*

● *The pains of the relationship with in-laws.* This whole question deals with the tension of establishing personal responsibility and a proper independence without breaching the relationship. Once again, we have to be very careful here that we do not just focus on mothers-in-law and women in general. We have to recognize that men have very severe hurts, most of all by being considered irrelevant and being ignored. The whole focus is all too often exclusively on the women in the family. This is going to be very hard to get at because a lot of men do not believe they have a right to be hurt.

- *The brother/sister, sister/sister, brother/brother relationships.* Once again, this occurs on any age level, not just while they are still little ones in the home or teenagers. There are many hurts that are carried into adulthood and damage the relationship years later because of what happened when they were growing up. Then, of course, there are breaches that occur over money, jobs, or whether they were invited to be godparents or invited to a particular party or whatever.
- *Grandparents, their adult children, and their grandchildren and the hurts they have experienced.* So often grandparents just feel used, only welcomed when they can provide something or on very intermittent and expected occasions.
- *Children who have been treated as burdens.* This one is absolutely essential for the well-being of the Church. We can remove this cancer that is in our parents' hearts. A child who is raised in a home in which he/she is a burden, even if treated with great self-sacrifice and generosity, is going to have a terribly damaged self-image. Once again, this is going to be a difficult one to surface and to get people to come to, because it is so prevalent and so consistent in our society that our children do not even know any other way for their parents to respond to them except as burdens and the source of continual self-service.
- *Orphans.* That word is not used very much anymore, but the fact is, being an orphan is just as much of an experience today as it was when the word was more commonly used. Somebody whose father has died, even if the person is grown up, is experiencing what it means to be an orphan, there are a great many things here that have to be sorted out and healings to take place: the anger with God which many people experi-

ence and do not know how to handle; those who have not allowed themselves to be angry at God; the feeling of desertion, of not being one's full self anymore, a sense of one's own mortality.

- *Children of divorced parents.* We must remember that these children experience a hurt that is continuing. Of course, the traumatic hurt of the divorcing process which might have gone on for a number of years before the actual separation remains presently operative. However, it is expanded and deepend in their present life experience. These children are desperately in need of healing and want to be addressed directly or indirectly through their parents. Healing the parents is tremendously important for the adults themselves and also for their children. A healing of the parents will cut off the continuation of the damage but the hurts the children have already experienced must be recognized and receive a response. By then children of the divorced are those of any age, not just little ones or teenagers. Until a healing takes place the harmful effects of a divorce can remain, even in the adult son or daughter.

- *Young singles.* This area deals with the loneliness that our young singles experience; the terrible pressures they are under and all the decisions they have to make; the criticism they face and the rejection they experience; the distrust that surrounds them, the envy, competition, and manipulation not just from the media, entertainment or restaurant industry, but from their own relatives and friends. The expression "Thank God It's Friday" should really be made to become a meaningful one in which they can thank God—not so they have more occasions to escape, but they have a real occasion to celebrate.

- *Men haters and women haters.* There is an awful lot of this hatred that we can experience in our parish. Of course it comes from hurts and the tragic distrust that builds up as well as from the resulting callousness and anger that is experienced.
- *Sickness in the home.* This can provide a tremendous swirl of all sorts of experiences among family members, topped off, of course, by guilt and a sense of being selfish because of resenting the person who is sick. This is especially true when it is a chronic sickness, most especially of a child (for example, Down Syndrome, or a child who has leukemia), and how the interactions of the family members very frequently leave a lot to be desired. Sometimes out of the pressure of taking care of such a sick person, burdens are placed on other family members, not maliciously but because there does not seem to be any other way to handle it.
- *Poverty.* Here we find the pains and agony of people who are under constant pressure as far as their bills are concerned, or those who suffer from believing they are failures because they are unable to provide for their children as they would wish. The there is the more drastic kind of poverty where there is truly physical deprivation, the lack of dignity they experience and the sense of worthlessness they feel in their lives.
- *The pains that our women are experiencing.* This is a tremendously important source of pain. We can make such a contribution to the Church if we can really make a special effort to heal our women, not to placate them, not to refuse to face into the injustices that are constantly attacking them, but to offer them true peace. Just as in all the other circumstances of inflicted pain we have come across, here we are not always going to be

able to solve the problem or even offer any kind of adequate compensation. But we can address the agony of soul women experience.

● *People who are experiencing a low level of affection, whether in the home, the convent, or the rectory.* Affection is tremendously important for the happiness and well-being of people. The vast majority of our people are simply not getting enough affection in their personal relationships.

● *Those who have experienced hurts from those in leadership positions in the Church—priests, lay leaders, or sisters.*

● *Those who have had a miscarriage or those who have lost a child.* The focus here should be on what we could offer, most especially concentrating on the lack of understanding on the part of the spouse. The spouse may seem unwilling to give support and to talk about what is happening inside, sometimes out of what seems the best possible motives. The pain of loneliness and desertion that occurs in the spouse that is experiencing this, the guilt that comes from the death of a child, the pain that comes from the bad, humanistic, and non-spiritual advice which is given on the occasion of such a death—all these are sources of great suffering. The classic case is the man who is trying to be strong so as to support his wife in her grief, but he comes across to her as callous and cold. She wants to talk to him about this and he always seems to be changing the subject. So she gives up and she does not believe he understands her.

● *Those who are in difficult marriages.* The basic causes of difficult marriages are, of course, masculine irresponsibility and feminine distrust. These problems express themselves in various overt and more subtle ways—the lack of listening on the part of the spouses, the focus on being loved rather than loving, the conflict of their value systems, the manipulation, the little fights and arguments, the digs and harsh teasing. We are not ignoring the more atrocious forms of difficult marriages where there might be abuse or alcoholism or infidelity or vicious levels of fighting, etc. People like that are certainly most open to come to the healing services we would establish. But sometimes we so concentrate on those extreme cases that we forget the vast majority of people are not in those circumstances, but rather in circumstances of a lower level of constant hurting and pain.

- *Those who are widows or widowers.* There is often the anger and the feeling of desertion. It may sound silly, but in fact many widows and widowers are angry at their spouses for having died and left them. Then they feel upset because they feel that way and they also feel anger with God. This situation often includes anger with the children for being a burden and distraction from the mourning, as well as an opportunity for wallowing in self-pity. There are pains and guilts in widowhood of not having said "I love you" often enough or not having gotten across to the person who is deceased how much he/she meant and so on. It is not just the loneliness which ensues once death has occurred in a family. But it is especially the recognition that I bypassed my opportunities because I thought there was more time.

This is by no means an exhaustive list of hurts, but it does give a sampling of people we can approach. Unfortunately, our attitude toward hurts tends to be very materialistic and physical. One of our difficulties, of course, is that we are so used to the kinds of pains that have been mentioned in the list we become numbed by them and do not expect that we can do anything about them. But we must remember that Jesus promised joy. It is very difficult to experience joy in the Church community when these types of hurts are being inflicted day after day after day. We can do something about them—the Lord has given us this power. That is what we have to believe because all of these are sinful and sins of relationship. We have a special charism in the Church to deal with them—the Church itself in its essence is about relationship and unity. Through the Church we can all become whole again.

2 HEALING: A CHARISM OF THE CHURCH

Healing is a charism of the Church, one that comes with the sacrament of Confirmation. We have to recognize that each of us has this power of healing. We may not believe we do, but actually the power has been given to us by the sacrament and we have allowed it to atrophy. That is why we do not recognize that we have it; it is rusty from disuse.

The Healing Church

It is very important to recognize that it is God's will that the Church be a healing Church. One of the best ways the Gospel is proclaimed is by healing. People will listen to the Church when it is obvious that healing takes place, both within our midst and from us. Healing is not an accidental thing nor is it a nice service that the Church provides. It is an essential part of the mission of the Church and of the identification of the Church. The Church cannot really be the Church without the power to heal being exercised strongly, frequently, and very visibly.

All of us in leadership in the Church have to recognize that we are sinners in this matter. By leadership in the Church, we mean those who have been particularly touched by the Church, such as bishops, priests, sisters, brothers, lay leaders and those who have employment in the Church. We need to reconcile with our people for having deprived them of healing. Consequently, since there is need for reconciliation, there is also need for reparation. We have to make a priority out of healing to make up to our people for what we have deprived them of over the years.

Healing and Confirmation

We have to connect healing overtly with the sacrament of Confirmation. It is not just some special people in the Church who have the power to heal, all of us have the power to heal. With some, it is more developed than others. Although healing is a special charism, the charism comes from the power of the sacrament of Confirmation. It is not separate from the sacrament. Very definitely the power to heal is part of Jesus' presence in our midst and our mission to witness to Him through true healing. The healing is not just for our sake; it is for the sake of the whole Body of Christ and its task in this world which is to establish the Kingdom.

The Charism of Healing

We have to understand that healing is not an aspect of medicine. The focus is not so much on the person healed; it is on the proclamation of the glad tidings. It brings forth an awareness of the power of the Lord and of His very definite presence among His people. If all we concentrate on is getting our difficulty taken care of or of caring for individuals who are hurting, and if the glad tidings are not announced in the very precincts of the healing and as a consequence of the healing, both in the healer and the person who has been healed, then we have missed the point.

Healing is not just a new thing in the Church along with some of the new rituals or the new forms of catechetics. This is something that has always been a power of the Church and always part of the mission of the Church community itself. It is not a social service type of experience with religious trappings. It is a sacramental experience, coming from the sacrament of Confirmation, and consequently an ecclesial experience. It should be part of the normal, standard way of living in the Church. It should not be considered extraordinary, but part of the normal life of the church.

What should cause us to strike our breasts in recognition of our sinfulness and build in us an awareness of the need for reparation, is that we have allowed healing to become something out of the ordinary, something that seems odd almost. That is like in a family where hugging and kissing is a once-a-year event or something for only special occasions. So the hugging becomes something tremendously overwhelming. That is not a good sign. The same is true of healing in the Church. We have to raise our consciousness on this matter and bring to the forefront the importance of healing as an ordinary experience in the Church. It should be ordinary to us in the sense of its frequency. But healing is not ordinary in its power to proclaim Jesus. In that sense it should be tremendously extraordinary.

An Act of the Church

It is important to be clear on what healing is. Healing is an act of the Church, not a personal power that is given to woman or man. Nor is it a direct intervention by God. It is always incarnational and through the Church. God has chosen to save people through the ministry of other people in His Church. This is part of the true meaning of the Incarnation.

Healing should be a normal part of our life in the Church. In any family we expect that there be food on the table, a roof over our heads, and that we have clothes to wear. Healing, too, should be as normal as that. This is not to suggest that healing should be as taken for granted as food, clothing, and housing. That way we would lose the sense of gratitude for those who provide the healing and a sense of wonder at the Lover that empowers the healing. But it should be expected and then in that expectation, the response of glorious gratitude and appreciation should be called forth.

A Fuller Life

It is essential that the Church be part of the real life of men and women, boys and girls who are its members. The Church has to be incarnational; it cannot simply be otherworldly. That has always been a tremendous temptation of the Church, that we raise the experience of Church beyond the normal life of people. Jesus came to proclaim joy and fullness of life to people. Being a member of His Body should lead to a fuller life in men and women that are members of the Church.

For too long the Church has been getting people to do Church things. It is time for the Church to do people things and become more significant for our people's daily lives. In a very real way, it is a fair question for people to ask: "If I become a member of the Church, how will it profit me? How will it make a difference in my life? How will I be better off?" That may sound selfish and materialistic, but the honest truth is that life is not divisible. Human life and material life and psychological life are just as real and just as much part of God's concern for us as is "spiritual life." Basically the question should be one that makes us in the Church face ourselves and see how real we are, how much like Jesus we are. Jesus walked among the people. He was like them in all things, save sin. So the Church has to walk among the people and be for them and make them truly experience a richer life. Only if we answer them first on their terms can they listen to the greater dimensions of life that we have to offer.

Furthermore, if we say that it is not a proper question or too materialistic to ask what the benefit is of the Church membership, what we are really doing is refusing to answer the question. We are putting the questioners on the defensive and making them feel inadequate or guilty. We have to look within ourselves and see who we really are. If we are not striving to make our people richer, then what are we about? Healing is something that can make our people incredibly rich.

The focus is on the profit to the Church, however, not just the well-being of the person to be healed. All charisms are given to the Church to proclaim the validity of the Church's claim to be the Body of Christ, the Proclaimer of the Gospel. The various charisms as mentioned in Scripture are given to nourish the faithful, to announce to those in the community and those outside it the glad tidings that this is the Church of Jesus Christ and that Jesus Christ is Lord.

The Sign of Healing

Without healing the Church of Jesus Christ cannot be believable and authentic. We simply do not give the appearance of being authentic. So the use of healing in the parish is not just to take away pain or to accomplish some good for an individual or small group of individuals. The focus of this charism is just as much *toward* the Church as it is from the Church. In a very real way, healing is an announcement, an attention gatherer, as is any miracle. It is a call to people to notice that there is something special here, not just another group of people, another religion. The power of God resides within us.

Healing gives credentials. It calls people to us. We provide healing for anybody who comes, of course, and we do not ask them to be Catholics before we would heal them. Yet after having been healed, they have to question whether or not they are called to join in our midst. If the healing just takes place without any invitation to become a permanent part of this community, then we are just doing good things for people because it gives us the satisfaction of helping people rather than offering the fullness of the message of the Lord to them. In a real way, such healing is cruel because it makes a promise that we do not fulfill. It promises a new life and gives them a fresh start by healing, but then we walk away from them and ultimately they fall back into their hurt or discover a new hurt.

Healing and Evangelization

Healing must be evangelizing if it is to be true healing. By evangelizing we do not just mean reaching out and serving other people, but attracting, drawing people in. Healing should bring about conversion—a true conversion of heart for those who have already been baptized and a call to Baptism to those who have not.

Consequently, one of the necessary qualities of anyone called to healing in the parish is a true love for and devotion to the Church. The healer first of all has to have a tender love for the faithful and see the brothers and sisters in the Church as people who are special. Without a really powerful experience of the virtue of love for the Church and its people, the work of the healer is not going to be very strong. In the healing the person healed is going to be manipulated or at least deprived of the fullness of the healing power of the Lord. So the healer must be immersed in the ways of the faithful in the Lord; otherwise, just the personal goodness of the healer is witnessed and we the Church are not visible. We have been called to reveal the Lord in our presence to people. But it is not our presence as individuals that is witnessed, but as community, as Church. If people who are healed do not experience Church, then the healing is very definitely deficient and inadequate.

3 HEALING TAKES TIME

Healing is a process. Like any process, it is normally going to take place over a period of time. Of course, God can accomplish anything He wishes so the healing is sometimes instantaneous, but normally that is not the way it happens. This is not because God is not willing but because we are not willing. We have barriers and resistances that prevent the healing from taking place.

There also has to be a predisposition toward healing; a lot of openness has to be created. Openness does not occur overnight. It is true that God can make His presence felt in an overwhelming way to an individual for specific purposes of His own and in order to call people to respond to Him in His Body, the Church. Nonetheless, we have to be conscious of God's normal way of operation. Grace does build upon nature. If we try to rush things, the net result is going to be disappointment at the very least. Furthermore, we risk inflicting further hurts through that disappointment.

A further dimension, which has even worse ramifications, is that when we go for speed, the focus is on the hurt and the alleviation of that hurt instead of proclaiming the glad tidings and God's presence in our midst. It is much more likely that the focus of attention is going to be on the human aspect of this whole action, especially on the healers, rather than on the divine. We may tend to think that might not be true. We may feel that if it happens instantaneously, then it is more likely that we will say the healing is beyond human explanation. But the problem is not God's power and the evidence of His presence; the problem is our willingness to accept His power and presence. We have to be disposed toward God, to work on our self-centeredness, pride, secularism, and lack of faith. In a very real way, the time factor is even more important for the healer than it is for the person being healed, although it is also tremendously important for him or her.

Importance of Establishing Personal Relationships

The reason for setting up a process is not to try to program God or to determine how He is going to operate. The reason for the process is to recognize the human dimensions of this experience and to make it gentler and more tender. It also gives us an opportunity to create a more personal relationship with those who come to us.

A very real part of the healing process is to get to know the individual man/woman/boy/girl who comes to us and to allow them to get to know us. Personal relationships do not happen overnight. We should really look carefully at any healing that is set up in the Church that does not call for a personal relationship. We are not saying that it is always wrong. What we are saying is the much better way to accomplish this healing, and a way to guarantee that the healing will have its full effects, is for a continuing relationship to be established between the healer and the person healed.

The Charism of Healing Is Broad-Based and Temporary

Something to consider seriously is how long someone who has been gifted with the charism of healing in accordance with the discernment of the Church should continue to exercise that charism. We could well imagine the possibility that as soon as the person runs out of capability of establishing an intimate relationship with those who are healed, then somebody else should be called forth from the community to take the healer's place.

There is much danger involved here. First of all, there is the danger of pride. The more powerful the grace given us, the more we have to be fearful of falling into the sin of pride. Pride, of course, comes in very subtle forms. It is not necessarily that the healers believe they are doing the healing by their unaided power, but they may believe in the parish they are the ones who most have this charism. We are not trying to control God here, to shut Him off or to say that He can only use a person for a restricted period of time. We are saying that in all probability, the charism of healing is much more broad-scale within the community of the Church than we presently accept it to be. In the average parish, a lot of people are likely to have this grace. Consequently, for that reason alone, we should be looking to expand our cadre of healers.

A second factor to recognize is that a far more important and greater grace even than the power to heal is the power to love. It is essential that we establish a love relationship of intimacy with those with whom we are in contact through the charism of healing. Nobody is capable of loving huge numbers of people with intimacy. Love is always the best antidote to pride. By the very restrictions that are evident in love, we can avoid the sin of pride. We must restrict ourselves to dealing with those with whom we can be intimate.

Another reason for having the gift and charism of healing on a relatively temporary basis is to make the Church's involvement in the healing much more evident. The longer one person is engaged in the charism of the ministry of healing, the more people will focus on that person. Even if that person is very holy and humble and responsive to God and gives God the credit, it can tend to be a non-denominational or gnostic form of healing and not a Church one. The ecclesial dimension is extremely important in this ministry.

Another factor, of course, in setting up a process that is time-consuming is that we are able to expose our people to more different personalities in the Church. We are not counting on just one person. Furthermore, there is peer involvement here. In this way we avoid the danger of our people coming to the healer as a magician and the danger of allowing the whole interfacing to be between the healer alone and the person healed. Instead, we want to establish a community dimension to the whole experience of healing.

Another factor is that in dealing with the healing of relationships (and that is the prime healing addressed here), we know that true healings can take place but they do not always last. People can have reconciliation with their parents, spouse, children, or with a sister or brother. The reconciliation can be real and sincere at the time but a couple of days or years later, it has not held together because we have not thought it through enough, we have not made plans, we have not built up the strength and courage and inspiration to live out the call that reconciliation gives. One of the things to get across in this whole process of healing of relationships is that there is a mission involved here. That mission is not just to proclaim that the Lord has healed me—that is very definitely a part of it—and not just to express gratitude and thanksgiving to Him, but also that because we have been healed, we have special powers now to deepen and tenderize the relationships which have been healed.

We have a special capability to step above any subsequent hurts and be more responsive to others in our life. But until I have an overview of our relationship and where the hurts have come from and how I have responded to them and what changes I have to make, the main focus is going to be one of intense gratitude and relief from the pain which has afflicted me, but it will not be incarnational enough and determined enough.

The Process of Healing

These are the steps in the process of healing:
1. I realize I am hurting.
2. I identify where I need healing.
3. I forgive the wrongs against me.
4. I show willingness to accept healing.
5. The healing itself.
6. Thanksgiving.

There are necessary steps toward a healing. They take place in that order. I cannot bypass them. Sometimes I want to get right to the healing, but that is not the way it will happen. In order to come to the realizations and decisions of this process, I must pray for God's help. More than that, I should ask the Body of Christ to pray with me and for me as I seek to be healed.

Since the process has six steps (as described above), the Body of Christ should pray that I succeed in each step in the process. This could be done at a parish prayer meeting where the parishioners break up into a number of sub-groups. Ideally there should be about six persons in each sub-group and there might be more than one sub-group for each step of this process. Often I am anxious to claim that I have accomplished each step of this process only to learn that I was deceiving myself and that I had not sincerely decided to forgive or to seek forgiveness. In order to avoid this problem, I must let the sub-group tell me when they observe that I am ready to move on to the next step in the process.

It may take me many times in one or the other sub-groups before I am ready to move on to the next step in the process. I cannot rush this process. I have to take myself where I am and continue from there. Others may be tempted to try to force feed me at this point, but it is not a question of how often I have had to attend the same sub-group but whether I have experienced the full grace that is there.

Healing as an Examination of Conscience

The interior dimension of healing has to be emphasized. Too often people approach healing experiences in terms of "What is the healer going to do for me? How is the healer going to make me feel better or take away my pain or help me cope with my situation?" In any healing process, I have to examine my resources and my deficiencies, and to see the ones I have not utilized or the ones I have not exercised properly. In many cases, the basic reason for my hurts is that I have not taken the graces that I have been given by Almighty God and put them to proper use. I have only used them when I felt like it or when I thought the other person in the relationship deserved or earned it, and it became a competitive type of thing. Naturally in competition between persons, both sides get hurt. Most of all, I have to come to grips with just how powerful I already am, what my true dignity is, and how much I am capable of accomplishing through God's grace which has already been bestowed upon me. It is not so much a question of discovering something new; it is more a question of a willingness to activate those graces that I have already been given.

I also have to face the deficiencies in my life, those graces I do not have because I have not sought them or I have not allowed God to give them to me, or that I have accepted only in very restricted measure. I have to discover how I have been resisting and what I am going to do about that resistance.

Humility in Healing

Above all, the quality I need most in order to receive a healing is the quality of humility. In a real way, it is like what they say about an alcoholic—until an alcoholic hits rock bottom and therefore is willing to admit not just that he drinks too much but that he *is* an alcoholic and it is his way of life, there is no possibility of a cure. The same thing is true for any kind of cure—until we admit that we need one and that we are totally incapable by ourselves, unaided by grace and community, of accomplishing our own cure, then it is not going to take place.

The example of the alcoholic provides a lot of lessons for us. The hardest thing for the persons to recognize within themselves and then to admit openly is the need for other people in their lives. Very frequently they are willing to accept God, and many of them pray very sincerely, and they make real commitments to stop. The old system of "taking the pledge" is a perfect example, but it does not work because they have to be humble enough to recognize they are out of control; they cannot accomplish it by themselves, no matter how determined they may be. They need to put themselves unrestrictedly in the hands of their brothers and sisters in the community of believers if a healing is truly to take place. All of us need that humiliation, we need to accept the humbling quality of that experience in order to be truly healed.

This is especially true, of course, when it comes to the healing of relationships, not just a healing of some physical ailment. One of the factors that we should really look at when somebody comes to us for a physical healing is to probe and investigate gently just what their personal relationships are like. Increasingly we are discovering that physical ailments are very much impacted by people's own image of themselves and that the level of their contentment with their life is more determined by their personal relationships, especially within the family, than by any other single factor.

Coming to Grips With Our Hurts

The first thing we have to get our people to concentrate on is the hurts they are experiencing. This means not just the hurts that are most immediate, the surface ones which cause them to come to us, that we have to get them to recognize. Many times, a wife's problem with her husband is rooted in a problem that she had with her father growing up. Or the wife is modeling her mother's conduct toward her father in her relationship with her husband. It could well be, for example, that a man's hurts with his pastor are merely another expression of what he is experiencing at home where he is not considered to be terribly important, just a nice adjunct to have around. The real hurt that has to be faced is between him and his wife. The pastor could make all sorts of changes and really seek a true reconciliation with his parishioners but it is not going to take place until the man's hurting experience with his wife has been healed.

So many hurts are interconnected; they reinforce one another. The net result is a cumulative hurt. We have to help people come to grips not just with the immediate hurt, the ones they are most aware of, but with the ones that foster that hurt and very frequently cause it. We are not talking here about depth therapy or analysis. We are simply getting people to talk about what goes on in their lives and helping them to become aware of the whole interlocking aspect of what they are going through.

Building Trust in God

If the person to be healed is truly disposed, God will not be outdone in generosity. On the other hand, as long as we are just focusing on the pain or the circumstances which cause that pain, we are not really allowing God to operate in our lives. Furthermore, we are not even conscious of God, but only of what is hurting us. God is only brought into it in terms of what He can do about my hurt. He is not significant in Himself. With that kind of mentality, we are using God and making Him our servant.

I have to approach God as my Father, with a tremendous love and responsiveness to Him. I have to be overwhelmed by His presence, get outside of myself, and allow Him rather than me to be the dominant person in our relationship. Once that happens, God can and does work wonders in us. But as long as I am the dominant person in my consciousness, then I am limited as to what I can accomplish (which is what brought me here in the first place). The fundamental problem that we have to come to grips with and help our people face is not God's willingness to heal. That is beyond question; it has been guaranteed. It has been proven time and time again.

Am I Willing to Be Healed?

The real problem is my willingness to be healed. That can sound funny, especially if I am undergoing so much pain. But doctors can assure us that there are many patients who are simply not willing to allow the doctor to function as a doctor. Many patients simply will not allow the doctor to heal them because they are convinced that they know better than the doctor, or that they have tried a particular remedy before, or the doctor does not really understand them, or they simply do not like the treatment the doctor offers. To be cured will demand of them a change of lifestyle and some very real sacrifices. They are not willing to change and would rather (odd as it seems) put up with the pain or sickness than make any significant change in their life.

Once again, the alcoholic is a perfect example. He knows what he has to do; he is simply not willing to do it. The pain he experiences and causes through his drinking bothers him, yes, but not enough for him to do what is necessary. The same thing is often true with ourselves in respect to God. What is going to block the cure and prevent God's grace from being operative is ourselves and our unwillingness to accept it, not because the grace is not there, not because it is powerful enough, but because we are simply not receptive.

So the concentration in the healing process is not to dispose God to heal, but to dispose the person to be healed. It is not to work on God, but to work on the person. It is not to change God's mind, but to change my mind and to create an openness in me. The purpose of these changes, of course, is not to dispose God toward me; it is to dispose me toward me and to prepare me for a healing. God is our Father; He loves us; He wants what is best for us, and He wants His children to be happy. That is why He sent His Son. That is why His Son said to us very specifically, "I tell you all these things so that my joy may be in you and your joy may be complete."

There is no question that God wants us to be happy, but we want to be happy our way. We want to be happy and still live the way we have been living. We want to be happy, but we do not want to have to change too much. We have to accept God's happiness that is His will for us without qualification or condition. Until we are willing to do that, then the healing is going to be as conditioned, as partial and as restrictive as is our receptivity.

Healing Begins Within

We cannot emphasize enough the absolutely essential dimension of helping those who come to us to recognize that healing starts with them. This does not mean that they can accomplish the healing by themselves, but they can block the healing by themselves. Until they are willing to unblock, they have tied God's hands. God simply will not intrude upon our free will; He will not take back the trust He has placed in us.

Mentality For a Healing Ceremony

If we are going to get involved in healing, we have to accept the comparison with alcoholism, especially when we are dealing with the healing of relationships. Our hurt is a condition, a way of life, and we are out of control. God cannot act on a soul that is not humbled. He does not force us; He offers us His grace. He does not overpower us with that grace. So it is essential for those who are engaged in this charism to have a very clear image of the participation they have to call forth from the participants in the healing ceremony. We have to have a tender love, concern, and care for the people who come to us and a vulnerability and willingness to risk rejection by helping them see that there are many significant changes that have to take place within them before any true healing can be affected.

All too often people come to a healing and want others (mainly the healers) to take away all the hard work necessary. Very frequently it is like that in the relationship to start with, the flawed relationship that is causing them the pain. They look for a husband, wife, or child to bring them instantaneous happiness and all the energy and effort has to be on the other person's part. The only work they put into it is when it pleases them. *The first focus of any healing ceremony has to be to change the mindset of the persons who have come for healing—to help them get the focus off their pain and into their potential, their interior resources and their willingness to use those resources, their willingness to change their pattern of behavior so that a healing can be accomplished.*

Is not this what Jesus meant when He said, "There are some devils that can only be cast out by prayer and fasting"? There is a very definite connection between the disposition of the person to be healed and the actual accomplishment of the healing. There are calls for changes of characteristics and patterns of behavior, of commitments, and of the practice of virtue before we will allow a healing to take place.

Too often what we really mean when we say we want to be healed is that we want the other person to be changed or we want to be toughened up so that if we have to make some changes they will be relatively small changes. Even if we recognize that serious changes are needed, it is only in the context of the other person changing as well. We have to pray for generosity in our souls—that we be willing to make the changes which are necessary for us to be healed, regardless of whether or not the other person in this hurtful relationship changes.

Healer as Lover

Another important factor to recognize is that teaching alone is not going to heal. Just giving people guidelines for relationship and describing the proper method of interaction between husband and wife or parent and child is not sufficient. That can be helpful but healing is not a parenting class, nor does it concern itself primarily with content transfer. That might be a minor part of this whole process, but it is not the prime factor. What we have to offer in the Church is a relationship with us. This is not just a relationship with community as a whole, but specifically with us as members of that community. The greatest healing is going to take place when we offer ourselves to be in relationship with those who come to us, not just as advisors or counselors, but as friends. In fact, we offer ourselves as more than friends—as brothers and sisters in the Body of Christ. Once we get that concept across and really start to practice it, the process of healing is well-advanced. It is this approach which is going to give people the self-image and self-confidence which will give them courage and strength to try again. It will help them to overcome the pain and to get through to the other person. Advice, even the most prudent and insightful, will not do that.

Virtues, not results, are what we are looking for. Too often we want to rush to the end of the process. We are looking for a magic solution to solve our problems or for God to take the pain away. We must recognize that this whole experience is to get our people to seek and accept the necessary virtues rather than aim directly at the healing.

A Note on Healing

Throughout this chapter we are talking about relationships that have some hope in them. We are not talking about pathological conditions, either on the part of the person who approaches us or the person with whom he or she is in relationship. What is called for in such cases is not a healing but a consultation with the appropriate mental health professionals. It is like somebody coming to us with appendicitis. We would not pray directly for the healing of that appendix. We might pray for direction and guidance to select the proper doctor. God does not usually intervene when there are normal, human means to handle the situation. So if there is a true and deep mental disturbance on the part of one or the other or both parties in the relationship, what has to be prayed for is an admission of that reality and a willingness to take appropriate steps to seek professional help. The healings we are talking about are the healings of relationships which have been damaged by sinfulness, by human willfulness and carelessness, by an unwillingness to be self-sacrificing.

That does not limit us much because one of the things we have to recognize is that much of what now seems to call for professional advice, direction, and help is really more a spiritual problem which calls for forgiveness, repentance, and healing rather than therapy. This is not being reckless. It is not ignoring that there will be some people who come to us for healing who are not primarily in the spiritual categories mentioned above. We have to have true prudence and know when to refer. One of the dangers today, of course, is that we just automatically assume we should refer. This is a way of ducking responsibility and avoiding the pain of a difficult healing process.

4 THE HEALING CEREMONY

Overview of Process of Healing

Exposition of the Blessed Sacrament
Presentation at General Session
Statement on Forgiveness
Meetings of Core Group and Sub-Groups
Return to General Session
Short Homily
Buddy System Explanation
Benediction
Kiss of Peace
Laying on of Hands (optional)

The concentration in each one of the sections of this healing process will be to create an environment and atmosphere in which the graces given to us by the Lord become part of our lives so that we accept and implement them. The method to be followed will be this:

I. Exposition of the Blessed Sacrament

It would be a very good idea to expose the Blessed Sacrament at the very start of the General Session and leave it exposed throughout the Healing Ceremony.

Reasons for exposing the Blessed Sacrament are these:

A. *The Eucharist must be made more prominent in our daily life.* Even those of us who go to Holy Communion daily soon forget after the Mass is over, and then revert to a "normal" way of life. Maybe the Eucharist helps us to be a bit more kind or a little bit less impatient or demanding on others. But basically for most, it is a half-hour with some minor spillover. We have to recognize, however, we are called to a *Eucharistic way of life*. Yes, the experience of the liturgy proper is terribly essential to our consciousness-raising, but we have to keep reminding ourselves about it during the day and allowing ourselves to see one another as members of a Eucharistic people and to respond to each other that way.

B. *We have to believe that the Eucharist can change our lives.* The Eucharist will do more than just improve the quality of our lives. It can radically convert us, but we have to allow the conversion to happen. We should go to the Eucharist with a fundamental question, "What has to drastically change in my attitude toward myself and toward my capabilities and potential, what habit of sin has to be more meaningfully and more successfully curtailed?"

C. *The Blessed Sacrament is another reminder that it is God who heals, not ourselves.* The only reason we have any power to heal at all is because He has chosen us. We are made His people and He has bodied us with Him. Whatever power to heal we have is His power, shared and exercised through us. We have none of our own.

D. *The Eucharist has healing powers.* When we talk about sacramental healing, we tend to think about the sacrament of Reconciliation or the sacrament of Anointing. There is no question there are very definite healing powers connected with those two sacraments. Maybe we do not allow that healing action of those two sacraments to take place as much as we should, but at least we recognize the presence of their healing power. Many of us miss entirely the healing power of the Eucharist. Often we go to the Eucharist for consolation when we really should be going for a healing. Above all, we should be going to the people of the Eucharist for healing. The Church itself, as celebrator of the Eucharist, is a source of healing. We cannot think about the Eucharist without thinking about the Church. The Eucharist is intended to feed us into unity with one another in the Church, the Body of Christ. Essential to unity is healing, for healing is essential to human life. So *one of the prime focuses of the sacrament of the Eucharist is its special capacity to heal.* This is true not only within the confines of the liturgy proper, but also in all our other experiences of the Eucharist such as in adoration of the exposed Blessed Sacrament.

The General Session now continues:

A. *Prayers and Songs of Praise Addressed to the Father.* It starts with a General Session of all participants present which begins with prayer and songs of praise, most specifically addressed to the Father. An intense atmosphere of prayer is to be created. The presence of God is what we really want to concentrate on. We want to do everything that will create an atmosphere and environment in which the overwhelming presence of God is experienced. This is not easy to do, because almost everybody who comes is going to be wrapped up in their own thoughts or concentrating on what we, the healers, are going to do for them. So the first thing we have to do is concentrate and call our people out of themselves. They have to let go, to take their minds off how they want to live.

We are trying to get everyone to concentrate their attention where it should be. In a way, it is like a young couple going out on a date. Each of them, during the date, tend to concentrate on how he or she is enjoying the date instead of whether the other is enjoying the date, thus finding themselves rather than the other person. What happens is they miss one another during the date. Another example is parents who are constantly thinking about the future and what is going to happen when their child grows up, and they miss the child's whole childhood. They simply do not enjoy that boy or girl just as themselves; they are constantly dealing with the child twenty years from now. We have to calm them down and get them outside of themselves.

B. *Why Pray to the Father.* We have to dispose the people toward the wonder of Almighty God and the beauty of His presence to us. That is more significant and more important than anything happening to us right now. God is the focus of our concentration. That is why the songs of praise are so important. We do that not just to get God's attention or because it is the right thing to do, but because it puts us in the proper frame of mind and heart. It creates a Eucharistic environment and atmosphere that is very essential, for that is really what we are called to be, a Eucharistic people, a thinksgiving people. Furthermore, the focus is on the Father.

There are two dimensions to that title, Father, that are very important:

1. He gives us life; we are totally dependent upon Him. The whole notion of dependency upon God is essential here, and the gratuity and wonder and power of His gift of us to us. There can be no greater gift that anybody can give than life.

2. It is relationship-oriented. When we think of "father" we think of family. We think of protection, warmth, tenderness, understanding, security, and above all generosity. It is in the context of relationship that true healing really takes place. That is why our focus is on God as Father.

We want to build up in all of us the concentration on the presence of God rather than on my problem or what I am going to provide for people to meet their problems. As healers we have to work just as hard on this as those who have come to be healed. It is easy for us to be so busy about what we are going to accomplish for them that we can bypass the most important experience of all, which is simply enjoying God's presence. Until we can truly enjoy His presence and just relax and luxuriate in it, we have not accepted Him as Father. We may have accepted Him as Omnipotent or even as Creator, but not as Father. As a result, we have not really discovered ourselves. Until we discover ourselves, we will not accept a healing. As long as I am concentrating on my problems or my responsibility (depending on whether I am the person to be healed or the healer) then God is just a peripheral figure in the healing. We must do all we can to shake ourselves out of our self-absorption, take away our self-centeredness, and just be for Him.

Consequently a great deal of prayer and sacrifice have to go into a preparation for the very gathering itself. We cannot just walk in cold to a group of people to be healed and begin. All that preliminary work of taking our focus off ourselves has to be done well ahead of time so that we can lead our people not to a new place but to where we already are.

C. *Prime Point of Prayer*. The prime point of prayer is to experience God. It is not to say or do the right things or to accomplish anything good. Too often the focus of our prayer is on whether or not we are doing it right. We are like a young girl on a date whose whole concentration during the evening is on whether or not she is acting as a proper date instead of focusing on her boyfriend. We can go to God in the same way, being so self-reflective that we miss the experience. The important thing that happens in prayer is God's part in it, not ours.

All the effort and energy that we expend in learning how to pray is really for the purpose of taking the blinders from our eyes and the hardness from our hearts so that we can enjoy God and rejoice in His presence. In the beginning, the hymns will probably be fairly loud and full-throated—and that is fine. We want to drown out the noise that surrounds us with heavenly words rather than worldly ones. But as we approach closer to the person of God Himself, our voices gradually still so that the hymns, prayers, and words become much softer and gradually fade out completely or, at best, remain as a gentle backdrop.

We cannot put a time limit on this process, because with some groups there will be a greater responsiveness than with others. By the same token there are also times when we ourselves are more disposed. But this is an essential dimension. It is not just an opening or an acknowledgment that this is a Godly thing that we are about and then we are going to get on with it. *We cannot go on until we have accomplished in ourselves a sense of God's presence.* That does not mean that every single person who is in attendance has to experience the overwhelming presence of God. We cannot guarantee that. But it does mean that this has to be a general experience and we have to tell our people that they have to be honest enough to continue the attempt to place themselves in God's presence. This is part of the process.

D. Role of Penance in Prayer. At this time we would recommend to people that they determine what penances they are going to perform so that they can be more responsive to God's presence in the future. One of the greatest weaknesses that we have with prayer today is that prayer and penance are almost totally disconnected. That is why our prayer is often flabby and very much marked by a "give me" mentality.

Penance is not a negative thing at all; it is a very positive thing. As in the case of somebody doing exercises to trim the waistline or tighten up flabby muscles, the value of it is not the exercise itself but the results which come from the exercises. The point of exercising is not heroic endurance; it is a healthy, attractive body. The point of penance is the same. It is not to see how much we can give up or how many hard things we can effectuate. *It is to create an open soul, to remove the flab caused by our selfishness and pride.*

We are going to have to do a job with our people on this, because penance is "out" these days. Interestingly enough, never has it been more "in" for secular purposes and never has it been more "out" in religious circles. So we are going to spas and practicing ridiculous diets, purchasing or renting all sorts of exercise equipment, spending a lot of money joining nautilus clubs, jogging to the point of exhaustion. But when we talk about penance in the Church, people look on it as if it was medieval. We might just ask ourselves how medical people might look on some of the antics that we allow ourselves to go through in other areas of our lives.

II. Presentation at the General Session

This presentation should be brief, but it is terribly important and has to be well-prepared. First of all, we have very clearly in our minds just what information we want to get across to our people and why. It cannot be just because it is good information and we want to get it across for its own sake. It has to be part of a process and be internalized in our people. Therefore we cannot overwhelm them with the sheer amount of information given out at once.

We should illustrate our talk with a personal example of the role of penance in our lives. We should share with them the interior attitude that we brought to doing any penance at all, why we chose the particular penance, whether or not that was a good decision made for the right motivation, and how it affected us.

The presentation team will be composed of prayerful and devout people who have experienced healing themselves. Their purpose is to establish clearly in the minds of the participants the spiritual principles of healing and to give powerful witness to the way they have been touched by the healing power of the Lord.

At each General Session a very few items should be presented well and clearly. This need not be done all at once, even though the members of the group will range from those who are new and others who have been coming for a while. We have to give the information which we think is appropriate for the largest percentage of the group at any given time. We can count on those who have been with us for a while to bring the others up to date if necessary. We can also trust that those who have been with us will more deeply internalize what is being presented and learn more from the repetition.

The presentation should be personal. What is presented should be shared not just because it is good or generally appropriate or very necessary. We have to know where our people are and what they need.

We should give our own personal experience of the points we are making. If we do not have any personal experience of the point, then we should not present it. We cannot just be giving examples from other people's lives. The points that are to be illustrated are the virtues, not the effects. We are not telling success stories so much as we are sharing our struggle to accept the presence of God in our life, or to humble ourselves, or to get rid of pride or whatever happens to be the particular point. This will get us out of the realm of being teachers and we allow us to become brothers and sisters, fellow strugglers in the pursuit of virtue.

Again, brevity is terribly important here. We do not want to get long-winded or give a lot of extraneous details. We are not trying to become prominent. We do not want people to go away filled with a consciousness, much less an admiration, of us. We are not trying to tell our life story. All we are trying to do is get them to dream along a little bit within themselves so they can recognize they have done this type of thing themselves, or at least they are capable of it. The important thing about a sharing is what goes on in the listener's mind, heart, and soul rather than whether it shows us off to our best advantage or fully explains us.

So we have to ask ourselves not just if this is true and real for us, but how is it going to affect them. In no way are we trying to imply that we should say something that is not our experience, just because it might be impressive or helpful. We have to be honest and real. But we must be selective about our particular experiences in order to help them more.

A. Basic Presentation

The basic approach that we should take to our sharing is first to state a particular point that has to be understood, such as placing ourselves in God's presence or the willingness to forgive. The sharing should continue:

1. *We should present our initial reaction* to that piece of information when it was given to us—what really went on, not just in our head but in the core of our being.

2. Then *the resistance that I experienced*. In almost all cases at least some resistance can be expected, maybe less in some than in others. But these are powerful divine facts that we are talking about and we are not going to take them on easily. So we are going to have at least some struggles and difficulty—maybe it is just that I did not think there was any resistance and it was only later I recognized it was there.

3. The next part of the sharing is *how I came to grips with my resistance*:

a. How I recognized the blocks and barriers within me.

b. What caused me to recognize my blocks and barriers.

c. What helped me get beyond the appearances of openness. That is the biggest barrier of all. We really think we are open. In a very real way, this is the most important grace of all, because until I accept the fact that I have barriers, nothing basically is going to happen.

4. The next aspect of the sharing is *what disposed me to get rid of the barriers.* This does not have to be high and mighty motivation. It might just be that the pain was so great that I was willing to do anything. Or it might have been that God broke through my defenses and I could not resist Him. We have to be very careful in saying something like that, because we can come across as having had a mystical experience or we can place the whole burden on God and lead to a quietism, i.e., that I do not have to move until God overwhelms me.

This may seem like an awfully long sharing. It does not necessarily have to be if we pare it down and get to the essentials. Often in our sharings, there is much unnecessary detail. We talk around things instead of getting to the point. We might jot down what we are planning to say and then ask ourselves what is essential, what really advances an understanding of what we have experienced and what is peripheral—and then drop the second part.

B. A Note to Presenters

It is very important that the presentation not be read. It is all right to take little notes up there, but if we read it, people will be turned off. Furthermore, if it is basic and rings true we will not need to read it. Also, if it is alive and is still part of a present struggle (and that is really what the sharing should be), we are not going to need notes.

Another very important thing is that *not every member of the team has to share on every point.* One member of the team might make the point and then another member (who has had the most vivid present experience) is the one who shares. We want to avoid having every point illustrated by a sharing from each member. In fact, (at least on some occasions) there is no reason why just one team member cannot make the whole presentation and the others do not even have to be up there.

III. Statement on Forgiveness

In all the General Presentations, no matter how many of the group have been present before, *at least a segment of the General Presentation has to focus on forgiveness. This is the core virtue we need.* Without forgiveness, nothing is going to move or change. There cannot be any healing as long as we are harboring bitterness and unforgiveness in our hearts. As long as we are rejecting, we will equally reject healing. This cannot be said often enough or powerfully enough. We are not suggesting that it be long-winded or consume a lot of time, but it has to be emphasized each time.

In the sharing on this point we have to bring out just where we are with forgiveness:

1. What our initial reaction was.
2. What was most difficult about accepting it and its truth.
3. What helped us begin the process of forgiveness.

4. How we recognized where we were not forgiving.
5. What sins in us most prevented forgiveness.
6. What virtues we most needed to pray for, and to work hard to accept, what acts or attitudes we most needed to do penance for, and how we are still working.

Above all in this section we do not want to sound like a "goody two shoes," or as though we "have it made." It has to be a "share our struggle" type of sharing. We bring out how we really have to fight our lack of humility, how we are capable of seeing ourselves as much more sinned against than sinning; how we hold grudges, even though we do not like to admit we are that kind of person; how we demand conditions before we will forgive.

IV. Role of Core Group and Sub-Groups

The healers then explain the general process of healing:

1. realization of hurt;
2. identification of need for healing;
3. forgiving wrongs;
4. willingness to accept healing;
5. the healing itself;
6. thanksgiving.

Then the healers discuss the various sub-groups and the core group that will be provided. They reflect on how the individual member is to discern which group he or she should join. We want to explain how they can make a good decision under the light of God's direction. They should join a group not because they are particularly interested in the focus of that group or because they think that group will accomplish the most for them. They should choose a group on the basis of where they discern themselves to be in the whole process of healing.

The primary focus is not on the group or the group's activity; the focus is on each person's present condition. (It is just like going to an exercise salon—the particular group that I would join would be the one that my physical condition most qualified me for. It may well be that I want the kind of figure that comes out of group X, but I simply do not have the muscles to participate in that group yet. I have to build them up.) I have to look at my spiritual muscles. I have to see what I am capable of and I cannot jump groups.

We then have to ask them to be prayerful about their selection and to allow the Spirit to guide them. Ask them to be truly humble and honest with themselves, to recognize where the Lord wants them to be and what is best for the Church. We should be emphasizing the Church here. When they are experiencing pain they cannot be as generous with the Church as they are when they are whole. Furthermore, it is almost an axiom that if I am hurting, I am also going to be inflicting pain. As a result the Church is damaged in two ways: first, I am less than who I can be as a member of the Body of Christ, and second, I am damaging the Body of Christ.

Another point that we want to make is that at least the first time they should join the first sub-group. Then people move on from one sub-group to the other on the advice, direction, and calling of the sub-group they are in. Moving on to the next sub-group is not a private decision. We want to build up an accountability here and we also want to get a Church involvement. It is the Church (meaning the people I am with) who call me forth from that group to go into the next group. That means that I have to be very open with my group and very humble and willing to accept their advice and direction rather than just taking my own direction.

The first decision that has to be made is whether I go to a group at all. Maybe I have to stay with the large core group because in all honesty I have not experienced God's presence yet. But once I join one of the sub-groups, then the decision to move on is made in concert with my fellow members in that sub-group rather than an isolated one. That is awfully important to establish. It takes the control away from us; it helps us avoid the tendency to delusion or to speed things up regardless of what reality is. It develops the community dimension of healing and my true dependence upon my brothers and sisters in the Body of Christ. It takes away the temptation to gnosticism and to the belief that God is a magician, and fosters in me faith, humilty, and openness.

Obviously, there is not going to be any enforcement in this; there is not going to be any rejection of somebody who appears in another sub-group on their own decision. We leave people the freedom of the children of God; we simply invite them to follow our directions and ask them to be generous enough and responsive enough to follow them. Then each person who wishes joins one of the sub-groups in a different area or room.

V. Meetings of Core Groups and Sub-Groups

Outline and mentality for both sets of groups are covered in separate chapters.

VI. Return to General Session

All the sub-groups return and join the core group community. As they enter, they are greeted with songs of happiness, joy, celebration, and gratitude to God for His presence in our midst and for our presence to one another.

VII. Short Closing Homily by Leader of Core Group

This homily should be inspiring, encouraging, and directed toward a deeper personal prayer life, penance, an immersion in sacred Scripture and the sacraments, and more involvement in the Church community. By that we do not mean people should be signing up for Church activities or organizations but they should be more immersed in the lives of the faithful.

VIII. Buddy System Explanation

Nobody should go home alone this evening. First of all, it is not good for somebody to be wandering around by themselves late at night even in the safest town or neighborhood. More important than that, we are denying by our actions what we are trying to accomplish when we let somebody wander off by themselves. They should be going home with somebody, and not just for that night. Everybody should have someone for whom they are responsible as an aid to their own growth and development as well as the other person's during the course of this week. We should set up a "buddy system" and have generous, good, and healed people available for those who have nobody to choose.

We should be very alert, careful, and sensitive to take care of the people who are more shy than others, the ones who are embarrassed to mention that they have not chosen anybody or nobody has chosen them. When these matters are settled, the responsibility of the members would be to be in touch with each other every day. This is not putting a burden on the leadership. We are not asking the leadership to make sure they contact everybody who comes to this healing service every day during the week between healing services. This would be setting up a form of clericalism, and it is also going to be a tremendous burden for the leaders.

We are not going to catch everybody in the buddy system. Some will refuse to do it, unfortunately, but we have to allow our people the privilege of failing. It is their right to choose, even selfishly and incorrectly.

We should also tell them that one of the reasons why hurts are so deep and long-lasting is we are enduring or fighting them all by ourselves. One of the reasons why we are sinners and do not accept the potential that God has invested in us by our sacraments is because we are too much on our own. Consequently, an important part of openness to the whole healing process is to accept a sponsor person or "buddy."

In a very real way, this is like the AA program, because anybody who joins the program has a buddy, somebody who is always at hand. That is what we want to establish. It is not that they just perform or get in touch with one another every day during the week, chat, and are nice to one another. That is not bad. But they have to be available to be called upon if the person's faith is ebbing, if they are starting to slip back into rejection again, or if they are starting to lose their humility and become more prideful, to lose their sense of prayerfulness and of the presence of God. We want to establish that they are to be close to one another, not just for the purpose of accomplishing a task or they are doing this because they are going to the healing service. But this is a necessary condition of them accepting God in their lives. this is part of being a member of the Body of Christ. Whether they are coming to a healing service or not, this is something which should be very real and meaningful to them. If they are really going to come to a healing, this is not just a nice extra. This is essential.

We do not want to lay out any formal outlines of what they are supposed to do with one another; we simply encourage them to be in touch with one another daily before the next meeting. They should pray a little bit with one another. They can do that over the phone as well as in person. They should share a little bit about their acceptance of God's grace in their life, where they are having difficulty, and how they need the other person's support and help. They should ask each other's advice on how they can forgive better, how they can accept the healing that has already begun within them, how they can improve the relationship that caused them to come in the first place, how they can have more strength and more power to overcome the barriers that the other people in their relationship are putting up, to accepting the change in them as a result of attending the healing.

IX. Benediction

The conclusion of the evening should be with Benediction of the Blessed Sacrament that takes place not just from the altar but by a procession among the faithful. After the final hymn of praise close with the Kiss of Peace.

X. Kiss of Peace

This "Kiss" should be a commitment to those that we particularly embrace. It is the beginning of the "buddy system." It should not just be a mass mob scene of throwing arms around people. We should be very selective and in giving the Kiss we should specify just how we are going to bring the peace of Christ to the person we embrace for this week or until we meet again.

It is very important that the Kiss of Peace be taken out of the level of pure ritual as just a nice practice by which we show how liberal we are and able to display affection in public. We have to restore its power, purpose, and meaning. It has to be a true commitment to those we embrace.

We can compare it with how a husband and wife embrace when they return home from work. Many times it can be just ritual, something they do because they have always done it, or they do it because she will get upset if they do not do it. Or they do it because it is a nice thing to do. All those are fine reasons; anything which gets them to do so rather than not is good. But there is so much more than that. Their embrace of one another should be a commitment to a tender, gentle evening. This sign of affection, warmth, and fondness should be a pledge for how the rest of the evening is going to be with one another. There should be true warmth to it. It is not done just for its own sake, but to establish a direction that we are going in with one another for the rest of the evening.

So, too, the Kiss of Peace should establish a direction that the two people who are embracing are going to go with one another for the rest of the week. This Kiss of Peace can be very powerful. It can be a tremendous corrective to the gnosticism so present in the Church, where we want a relationship with Jesus alone, but we do not want a relationship with one another. It can help some very real resistances in our people and can help them to identify where they have to change before they are capable of accepting a healing. It can begin the process of establishing a true community in our parish rather than just people who are celebrating a common liturgy together.

XI. Laying on of Hands (Optional)

At least on some occasions it might be a good idea to impose hands upon people, either in the small sub-group or in the larger group when they return after finishing their time in the sub-group. This should be done with the notion they are being commissioned to go forth to love, they are going in the name of the Church to establish their sacrament of Matrimony, or their parenting or their vocation as an adult son or whatever. We have to externalize these things. It is terribly important that these things not be just conceptual but instead be very visible and deeply felt. There are so many ways we can raise our people's consciousness and, most of all, raise our people's sense of their own worth, dignity, and importance in God's plan and in the life of the Church.

A Note to the Reader

We should be establishing a prayer power throughout the whole community, calling upon everybody we know who has a capability of great prayerfulness, to back us in this effort of healing. Most especially this includes our children—children have a great power of prayer, a great seriousness, intensity and openness about it. They can be our richest resource. Too often the children are looked on as having to be taken care of rather than as people who can make viable contributions to the Church at large. (It might be noted here that we certainly are not putting an age restriction on those who are participating in the healing community. The Spirit blows where He wills and there is no guarantee that somebody has to be 35 years old in order to be a healer. Who knows, he might be 10! We are not trying to suggest the likelihood of this, we are simply being open to it. But certainly, among those who are teenagers—most especially among their peer group—they can have great powers along these lines.)

5 CORE GROUP AND SUB-GROUPS

A core community, preferably made up of those who have already been healed, should remain in the main section after the Presentation continuing prayers of praise, thanksgiving, adoration, and intense petition for our brothers and sisters in the sub-groups. *The core group is absolutely essential to the healing process, not a luxury.* It is not just a nice way to bring people back who have been healed. Nor is it a way to keep people occupied while the real work goes on. The real focus of God's power is going to be in this core group. God's presence is going to radiate out from this core group into the sub-groups.

Core Group Format

The format of the core group can vary from week to week, as the meetings take place. In general, its composition should go somewhat along these lines:

A. *Hymns of praise and thinksgiving.*
B. *Testimony of how God has acted in our lives from participants in the core group.* The emphasis of this testimony should be on the experience of God, rather than the particular thing that happened. We want to share our relationship with God more than the effect of that

relationship. The effect is only important insofar as it reveals the relationship and our acceptance of God's presence in our lives. This testimony should be spontaneous and called forth from people, but we should explain very carefully what we want.

We do not want people getting up and giving us a report of their week or their pious practices. *We want them to share their internal experience of how God has entered their lives and what that has done to them. Not what it has done for them, but how they are changing. Part of this testimony is their specific need to be more open and to plead with the community to support them in this,* not just with their prayers, but with their active involvement in their life. In a very real way, this testimony should be an account of conscience, giving accountability over to this community.

C. *Prophecy talk.* This entails a talk by some member of that core group who has been healed, not necessarily by the leadership, but some person who has been coming to the core group on a regular basis. The talk should be on aspects of healing that are tremendously important for all of us to truly accept into our lives, not just into our heads. Some of the titles that would be recommended:

1. *The power of prayer*—not the goodness or necessity of prayer or how to pray, but the incredible capacity that we have because God has graced and empowered us with the gift of prayerfulness. The talk should include what that can accomplish in our own lives and in the lives of those we commit ourselves to with love.

2. *The community dimension of healing*—Healing is such a spectacular occurrence and in a way "distracting." God's power and presence is so overwhelming in healing that we can forget that it is within the context of His chosen people that He makes His power evident, and it is for the sake of the credibility of His people as chosen that He acts in such an overwhelming way.

3. *Penance and its power in our life*—for ourselves and for the community and for our loved ones.

4. *The Body of Christ*—what it means to be brothers and sisters with one another as the flesh of the Lord; the struggle it takes to live that way and the meaning, potential, and wonder of this reality.

5. *Sin*—specifically living sinfully, not just performing sinful actions, engaging in improper conduct or omitting some of the things which are our responsibilities; how we retain our sinful anger, our hatred, our refusal to be reconciled. We must see that the whole Church is wounded through our sin, its credibility stripped away. How the fundamental sin is divisiveness, expressed by the false conviction that I am right and others are wrong. How sin attacks the whole possibility of belief in our being the Body of Christ. How Jesus is not unbelievable; the Church is and is made so by sin. We make the Body of Christ a sinner when we sin. How sin is anti-healing; as long as sin is present and enhanced, healing is impossible and pain and rejection are inevitable.

6. *The acceptance of Jesus as personal savior*—not just the intellectual acceptance that Jesus is God and that He died for the sins of humankind. Instead I must concentrate on my personal relationship to Jesus—how much He is in my life, what that does for me, how it affects my decisions and relationships, and how, if I lose my acknowledgment of Him as my personal savior, that affects me. What I can do to change my heart.

7. *The danger that we concentrate on results*—We are praying and yearning for our people to return from their sub-groups, and we are looking for the high that healing will give us. We want to see who was healed so we can go home happy that we spent our time well and profitably. Then we can talk to our neighbors tomorrow about this miraculous event. That is just it—we are going to talk about a miraculous event instead of the Church as the Body of Christ and the wonders that occur in our community. The danger here is that this can be made to appear as magic or just emotionalism and humanism, while the whole point of healing is to call forth from us a deeper recognition of God's presence in our midst and our responsiveness as His people because of His choice of us. Implicitly, we can be claiming credit because we are doing such a good job of setting up this healing process, that we are praying so well. *It is God who heals; He heals so that people acknowledge Him as Father and recognize the Church as the Body of His Son.* Both of those dimensions are essential. Even if we recognize God as Father but do not recognize the Church, then we really have not accepted the true message of the healing.

8. *The danger of focusing primarily on the person healed, not on the Church*—How we can focus our attention in the wrong place: on the person healed or the marriage problem solved or the healed family relationships of parent and child, brother and brother, sister and sister. Surely these are important, but do they lead us to be more Eucharistic, more ecclesial? Does the healing result in bringing people closer to Jesus and to His Body, the Church? If not, then we are settling for too little.

9. *Sacramental life*—The presence of healing should be a call to deepen our sacramental experience of our brothers and sisters in the Church. Therefore, it should increase the frequency and above all the fervor of our celebration of the sacraments, especially of Eucharist and Reconciliation. It should also call us to be more open to the conversion experience of the Church.

10. *The notion of accountability to the Body of Christ for a whole way of life, and most especially for our relationships*—We report the condition of our souls and our willingness to accept our vocation in the Church. Our relationships are missions from the Church and therefore, we are responsible to the Church and its members for the way we live out that mission. Our relationships are not just for our own well-being and for our own interests and pleasures. Therefore, we have to place ourselves under direction and accept the prophetic voice of our people guiding and prodding us, showing the way, correcting us, and encouraging us.

D. *Prayers and songs of praise to our Father.*

E. *Response to prophecy.* One or other member can speak out in testimony before the whole group of how they personally have been affected by the prophecy. The focus of this, of course, would not be that they were impressed or that they learned something. The sharing would be in terms of how God is moving within them, how they are responding, and what changes they are going to make as a result of the prophecy given. Prophecy always calls for an active response, not just one of whether or not I agree. But what am I going to do about this call of God that has been expressed through my sister or brother? This is a very important part of the core meeting. Too often great prophecies are spoken but they remain sterile because there is no response to them. Or when they do take effect, it is only the effect on individual members, not one shared with the community.

We must do everything we can to establish the community dimension of this whole experience. We are not individuals chosen in isolation. We are chosen people and we do not belong directly to God but belong to the Body of His Son. Our acceptance of that call is more determined by the relationship that we establish with one another than any other single facet. *As part of the sharing, the rest of us can respond how we are going to support the individuals responding to the prophecy and how we are going to assist and aid in their living out the acceptance of the prophecy.* Accountability has to be a two-way street and the community has to be involved in the one who is making him/herself accountable to us.

The core community who are praying, celebrating, prophecying, and witnessing during the course of the sub-groups is an essential dimension. The Church needs to be visible. Unfortunately, without that core group, what will tend to happen is that the only participants are those who are either leaders or people who are in the process of being healed. So it becomes a ministry rather than a love relationship. It becomes something that individual good-willed people do out of the generosity of their hearts for those who are suffering and the Church is lost sight of. It becomes a service, a response to problems rather than a call to community. True, the pain has to be taken care of first and the healing has to take place before those healed can really exercise their part in the community. But the community has to be visible right from the very beginning of the process and an intimate essential part of it.

Take a simple case from everyday life. If I introduce you to your wife, you are going to have gratitude in your heart toward me all your life long and I am going to be particularly welcomed into your home. So too, if the Church introduces them to a healing, it is the Church that gets the credit and that is what we want. We want the Church to get the credit, not just individual members of the Church who happen to be particularly good. Otherwise, we as leaders are going to attract the gratitude to ourselves rather than to the Body of Christ as a whole. So the core community has to be very much part of this process and their role made very evident to all the participants. In a very real sense of the term, that core community has to have the dominant note of the meeting; the sub-groups are sent out from the core group and return to it. The core group is not just another sub-group on the side, doing one or another of the tasks in the process of healing. The core group is representative of the whole Church; it missions the people and welcomes them home. It is to this group the others are accountable.

The core group is also a guarantee to people that they are not going to be left alone. They do not have to have a problem to be important to us and for us to care for them. They are not left on their own again as soon as they are healed. That would be really cruel and inhuman. It is also a cause of great immaturity in the Church because it leads people to feel they must have problems in order to get attention. Yes, the problems and pain are real and we have to respond to them, but the focus of our life as Church is not to discover who has the greatest pain and how we can relieve that pain. The prime focus of the Church is to create community so that pain never happens in the first place.

People are called to experience and live out the full joy and enthusiasm of the community in which healing is given. The healing is not for its own sake or for the sake of the individual alone and in isolation. The healing is given to allow the individual to be able truly to love—something they cannot do while they are hurting and concentrating on their hurt. Pain takes away the freedom to be truly aware of and responsive to other people. Healing makes us free.

The Three Sub-Groups

The people who feel the need for specific healing for themselves or others and feel ready to join one of the sub-groups should do so. There are three major types of sub-groups and within them there any number of sub-groups may exist. The type of sub-group is determined by its purpose or focus. Sub-group I is aimed at the specific virtues of humility, contrition, compunction and forgiveness. Sub-group II focuses on my hurts and where I need healing. Sub-group III is concerned with the healing proper.

In the first sub-group, a basic question is asked to begin the process of sharing under the power of the Spirit and the searching for the particular graces sought. The question, the initial question, is just that—an initial question. The person who has one of the charisms or who has been healed in the past who leads this sub-group should be introducing other questions to go deeper and to keep the sharing going more powerfully. If the process bogs down and people seem blocked, the group should stop and pray even more earnestly for God's help. For a start one might ask, "How do I feel about the gift of tears? Have I ever cried for my sins?"

In trying to identify where I need forgiveness and healing, the question might be, "What characteristics in me do people find difficult to take?"—characteristics such as anger, jealousy, manipulation, control, independence, etc. What we are trying to do with this question is to get people to focus on their failures rather than how they have been failed.

In seeking for the virtue of forgiveness a question such as the following might be used: "Do I feel ready to forgive the person or persons who have hurt me? Do I really wish to give up my hurt?"

In each sub-group, as we said, there might be one, two, three, ten little groups. We do not want the small groups, the sharing groups, to consist of more than five or six people, including the leader or facilitator. Otherwise it gets too large, leading to a discussion rather than a sharing.

Whoever is the leader has to recognize that he or she is there only to ask questions and to provide encouragement for people to search within themselves rather than to provide answers. The answers have to be internalized. They have to be discovered by each person within himself or herself and cannot be given from without.

6 SUB-GROUP I: VIRTUES NEEDED FOR HEALING

Four virtues are essential to the process of healing: humility, contrition, compunction, and forgiveness. These are the focus of the sub-groups as each group strives to help people to prepare themselves for healing. The first virtue sought by sub-group I should be *humility,* followed by *contrition, compunction,* and *forgiveness.* The chief disposition the members are striving for is compunction and this should lead them to seek forgiveness as sinners.

Virtue of Humility

The focus is on the hurts I have inflicted, the barriers that prevent me from accepting healing. If I concentrate on how I have been hurt and turn inward on myself, there will develop in me a lot of self-pity and a demanding attitude. I will feel that because of my pain "I'm owed this." Pride and the independence involved rejects the possibility of my being open to God's presence. The hurts I have inflicted are a better focus for me—the unresolved hurts, the ones where there has been no reconciliation with the person involved. The best ones to recall are the ones I am presently inflicting. We want to take the attention off the "poor-me, how-badly-I'm-hurting-and-how-badly-I've-been-treated." There is no real possibility of healing as long as I am focusing that much on myself and on my hurts. I am always going to find more hurts—the very thinking of them with that kind of intensity deepens those hurts and makes them more vivid and more painful.

Making Room for God

The point we are trying to establish here is not that because I have inflicted hurts, I do not have any right to have any hurts of my own. We are simply trying to provide an environment in which healing can take place. One of the first steps toward that atmosphere is to recognize the hurts I am inflicting myself. Humility is necessary to allow God in. Until I have *humbled myself*—and those words are deliberately chosen—I am not being open to God. The truth is, when we talk about being humble, we usually mean we are embarrassed. Humility, like pride, is home-grown. Real humility is reality. I am never going to accept the power of God in my life unless I am a humble person, open to God and His action in all parts of my life. No relationship or part of my life can be marked Out of Bounds to God.

Furthermore, we need perspective. Our hurts are so alive in us, we become callous regarding the hurt that we inflict. Any hurt we inflict when we are concentrating on ourselves seem to us so minor compared with what we are experiencing. Those hurts become the most obvious thing about us—we establish all sorts of nonverbal ways and patterns of conduct which act out our hurts. We become cynical or suspicious or very careful in our relationship with other people, or very aggressive and demanding of our rights or hypersensitive to the intentions of others, etc. The result is, we are setting up a situation where others in our life are constantly reacting defensively, either getting aggressive themselves or suspicious, cautious, or very picky. That type of reaction on their part reinforces our hurts and adds to them. Then the focus of our relationship with the other people in our lives is in terms of our mutual hurts. And so we are constantly reacting to each other in terms of them.

Putting Others on Guard

Until we give true attention to how we are hurting, we will constantly put those close to us in a position of having to be on their guard against us or keeping things on a shallow level and avoiding anything that could trigger us off or of giving up their personal dignity in abject surrender to us before we are going to be satisfied. They will know by the aura we carry with us what lies in store. They are in for a fight or for coldness; or they have to agree with us or we will take it personally; or they have to prove to us their love. Then nothing they do is ever enough. They cannot be themselves any longer; they always have to be walking on eggshells in dealing with us.

Lessening Self-Righteousness

Being aware of our sinfulness is a very positive thing because it lessens our self-righteousness; it gives us a bit of compassion, and a more balanced view—rarely in non-pathological personal situations is the hurt and fault one-sided. We can accept that as an intellectual statement and realize it is true, but deep down in our hearts, we really believe, even if it is not totally the other person's fault, we are the ones who are really being abused and suffering the most. We have to start becoming aware of the suffering we have imposed, not so that we can compare the two sufferings, but because we are really good people and we honestly do not want to inflict pain. But when we are under pain ourselves, we simply ignore the pain we are causing and it simply does not get to us. We have to allow it to get to us.

This will be hard—the small group leader in the sub-group will have to be gentle but firm. People will want to excuse or justify themselves, try to get allies or approval from the other members of the small group. They might even feel betrayed; after all, the reason they came to this healing experience in the first place was because they were the offended party. They thought the emphasis and focus of the evening was going to be on making them feel better or at least receive some kind of compensation for their pain or a plan on how to get out of it. Actually, we are giving them a plan on how to get out of it: the first step of that plan is to face their own sinfulness.

Pain I Inflict

The leaders should not argue or try to prove persons wrong, much less to condemn them. It is so human and understandable that when we are hurting we are very self-centered. So the leaders should accept with understanding what has been said and bring the sharing back to the question which has been asked: "What are the biggest hurts I have brought to the relationship" (the one for which healing is being sought)? Point out that it is not important that the other person is worse and has inflicted more damage—that could well be true, but it is irrelevant. Simply point out in a gentle way that each one of us has to acknowledge and come to grips with not only the pain I am experiencing, but the pain the other person is experiencing because of me.

Need for Patience and Humility

But recognizing that truth intellectually is not sufficient. The person to be healed has to be led carefully and prayerfully to feel the other person's suffering deeply and meaningfully. It is not enough just to recognize that I have done some bad things. I have to feel for and with the other person. I have to feel so deeply that I am embarrassed and ashamed of myself. Only when I become ashamed of myself will I get off the hurt I am experiencing. The sense of shame is a sign that I have finally begun to feel with the other person and to experience a bit of what I have put them through. So a sense of shame is a very important interior reaction for us to call forth in the person that is in the group we are leading.

The leader has to exercise great patience with each individual in the small group—not expecting each one to respond equally well or at the same pace. There is a great temptation to do this; it is our bureaucratic mindset. We have to allow the Spirit to operate where and how He will and we are not trying to get a group healed, we are trying to provide the occasions for each individual to accept healing. That is going to take place at the Lord's pace and at the individual's pace. This is one of the reasons for the smallness of the group so that the leader can act personally with each member of that subgroup.

Nonetheless, our temptation is still going to be to want to come out with everybody having profited equally. That is not going to happen. If we try to force people into this, we are producing one of three different reactions. We are going to produce a "least common denominator" type of situation where some will be deprived of a fullness they should be experiencing. A second result is that we are going to get people to fake it, consciously or unconsciously. Because they feel it is expected of them, they are going to say they are experiencing it when often they do not even realize what they are supposed to be experiencing. A third and final reaction is that people are going to feel they are failures because they are not experiencing what is expected. So the leader must take it gently and understandingly. There should be no rush here. There is no standard which has to be met. Everybody is going to profit immensely just by being part of this little group.

The Lord's Work

There should be much prayer, much quiet listening to God gently being in our midst, caring for us, calling forth our best. Most of the time should be spent in a spirit of prayer. This has to be the Lord's work, not ours. The leader is there as creator of an environment and as one calling forth from us a desire to make God present to ourselves. He or she is not to accomplish this spirit of self-revelation and self-recognition in the individual participants, or course. Only God can do that with the cooperation of the individual persons. So the leader keeps the focus on target and keeps the question clarified, understood, attended to and, above all, keeps the concentration on God and God's work among His people. But the actual work is done within the soul of the individual person by the Spirit.

One of our temptations, of course, is that we cannot stand silence. Sometimes silence is absolutely necessary for the Spirit to accomplish His work. We should not feel that we always have to be talking. Sometimes people need the occasion to come to grips with themselves, especially in the presence of the Lord.

The leader, while in no way exhibiting any rejection, must establish the principle that discovering our sinfulness is a Gospel call, not a psychological thing or just a human thing. It is not just a good idea, but a necessary requirement coming from the Gospel itself. This is an important dimension to emphasize. We really have to come across to the people not just as nice people who belong to the Church, who are doing a good thing for them. We are really proclaiming the Gospel and it is the glad tidings of Jesus Christ that asks them to face into the question of their sinfulness.

Virtue of Compassion

Compassion is a virtue that is tremendously needed in the hearts and souls of the people of the Church. Without compassion, we will not be able to accept the healing power of the Spirit. It is not just that we need to be compassionate so that we avoid sin and so that we can understand people. We need to be compassionate for our own well-being and so that God can operate within us as He wills. We will not share the fullness of the kingdom unless we are compassionate. It is not just that we will not be good enough to other people or that we will not live up to our responsibilities. We will not live up to our opportunities. God cannot give us the healing that we need unless we have been gentled sufficiently by compassion to accept the healing that God has in store for us.

Our Refusals to Love

Our greatest suffering, after all, comes from our hardened hearts. We have decided to handle hurt our way, with the normal human reactions of rejection, closing off, building up indifference, inflicting hurt in turn, being hopeless, and marked by cynicism or sarcasm. The only way to pare off the callouses that we have grown is to become conscious (very deeply) of how we have refused to love. This is a real step in the process of letting go our hurt. In a very real way, it is like having a cut on your hand and you have closed your fist in order to protect the cut from getting dirty or to protect it from further exposure to more damage. When you go to the doctor you have to be willing to unclench your fist so he can get at it to clean it, put medication on it, and bandage it. No matter how good or sincere a doctor he is, you simply have to cooperate by opening your hand. We are not saying that by opening ourselves we accomplish the healing—we don't. But by opening ourselves we allow the healing to take place. The same thing is true as far as our relationship with Almighty God is concerned. We are preventing the healing that He wishes for us. Until we open up, the process of healing cannot go on.

The length of time any individual is going to have in spend in this particular sub-group will be determined on how prideful and hardened he/she have made themselves because of their reaction to the hurts in the relationship they have experienced. The only way they are going to give up their pride and hardness of heart is by becoming aware of their sinfulness. We are not trying to put them down. It is not a negative type of thing at all, but a very positive thing. It is taking the first necessary step toward creating an accepting heart, so that healing can occur.

Compassion means I am more aware and responsive to the pain I have caused than the pain inflicted upon me. Scripture speaks of Jesus' heart being filled with compassion. He had compassion on His people. So I am called to have compassion for my wife or husband, for my son, mother, or sister and so forth. It is a real virtue that is the foundation of humility.

Virtue of Compunction

The third virtue to be sought by the sub-group is compunction. Compunction consists in a deep sense of unworthiness, not based on self-rejection but on the goodness of the other person. Until I can truly see the other person's goodness, I will never see how bad are the hurts I have inflicted on her or him and what a real sinner I am.

The leader is to point out that as long as I keep my focus on what has been done to me, the net result is a judgmental and rejecting heart, suspicious, distrustful, and unyielding. These are the normal and ordinary consequences. Such a mentality builds up within me a sense of the other person's unworthiness, how much I have suffered because of him or her, how much better I deserve from them. This obviously is not something that is going to provide much of an impulse toward reconciliation. Pettiness of soul develops, a mean spiritedness, a desire for revenge, coldness, and withdrawal.

Rather, the Gospel way is to see the other person's goodness, to make that reality so much clearer in my mind than their faults or what I have experienced negatively. So the net result then is that I build up in my mind my unworthiness, how much suffering I have caused and how much better the other person deserves from me. Linked with my consciousness of how much pain I have caused develops a Spirit-led sense of unworthiness in me. We are not talking here about a pathological personality. The people who are coming to the healing are fundamentally healthy people, good and sound. They are fine people who, in their humanness and sinfulness, have developed deep hurts in one another. Also, we are not calling people to see their unworthiness when they look at their spouse, brother, or mother. We are not putting them down or causing self-rejection. The sense of unworthiness we are attempting to stimulate here is of the sanctifying kind—one that comes from looking at the other person's goodness rather than at myself. The unworthiness, therefore, is reflective rather than direct. I am unworthy not because I am so bad, but because the other person is so good. It is an uplifting type of experience, leading to appreciation of the other person and a greater urgency to live up to the other person's goodness and to be truly responsive to his or her worth.

Not Putting Down Self

Self-condemnation is not compunction. Self-condemnation is not going to help either party in the relationship. It does not lead to a greater capacity to love, but to withdrawal, a putting down of self, bringing the other person down to my level, a critical spirit and a loss of hope.

It damages the person who engages in it and he or she in turn damages all around him or her.

On the other hand, the unworthiness called for in this part of the process is based on a gentle heart and a magnanimity of spirit that helps us to be awed by the beauty and worth of the other. The concentration is very little on me and very much on the other person. So it is not that the other person is so good because he or she puts up with so much from me; but that the other person is so good. Until I can recognize that, I will not be able fully to forgive. Then the healing I seek will be my healing rather than *our* healing. It will be to take care of me instead of restoring *us*; it will deal with the symptom. At best, it will be a pain-killer rather than a return to full health.

So the leader of the small group really has to have a strong, loving heart. Our temptation is going to be to face into the pain rather than to face into the cause of the pain. It is like somebody who has been in an accident who is brought to the hospital. He or she has severe lacerations around the face and internal injuries. The doctor is going to treat the internal injuries. Very frequently the patient's relatives are going to be all worried about the scars on the face. But there is not going to be any life for that face unless the internal injuries are taken care of. The same thing here. The internal virtues have to be taken care of rather than the externalization of the pain. We have to get people to face into the necessity to forgive if they are going to be healed.

Other qualities of the virtue of compunction are, according to St. Ignatius Loyola, shame, confusion, the gift of tears. Sins are hardly ever all on the other side. I have to come to grips with the sins I have inflicted. No comparisons are allowed. I cannot say, "Well, my sins are there but they are minor compared with his sins or when you look at what she's done to me." As long as I am comparing, I am really not facing into what I have done.

Seeing the Goodness of Others

One of our most frequent failings, especially when we are undergoing pain, is that we look at the mote in the other person's eye and, of course, it appears gigantic to us. Then we effectively declare ourselves innocent because the other person is more guilty. Even if the other person is more guilty, that does not make me any less guilty. What happens is I reverse the whole call of love. Love is a call to discover the worth of the other person. Instead, I am discovering the lack of worth of the other person—at least, what I judge to be their lack of worth. But the whole focus of love should be to cause the other person to grow in their own eyes by seeing themselves in my eyes. That is what my real sin is, that I have allowed the hurt within me to turn off my potential to help the other person I claim to love become more aware of his or her own goodness and value in the eyes of God.

My life is to be improved, not so much by what is done for me, but by my recognition of how blessed I am to belong to this wonderful mother or father, uncle, spouse, grandparent, or child. I should have a thank-filled heart that I have this person who gives me his or her love.

Compunction, therefore, is a big-league virtue, one of great strength and power. It is a tremendous grace, not something we can accomplish on our own or even want to. The truth is, the whole notion of compunction, very frequently, turns us off and we even question whether it is a virtue. We go through all sorts of intellectualizing about whether compunction is just something medieval. So maybe the first thing we have to pray for is not the gift of compunction itself, but to unblock our hearts and open ourselves to the recognition that it is a grace. Only when we accept the goodness of compunction will we ever ambition to accept it as a gift from God.

Four Steps Toward Compunction

The whole question of accepting the grace of compunction is a process, not something that I can just have happen instantaneously. There are four steps in this process of becoming a person with compunction:

1. *To consciously and deliberately bring God in*—It is not merely a human gift or capability, but something that comes directly from God and only from God.

2. *To face into whether or not I am willing to accept the grace of compunction*—Presuming God is willing to offer it to me in overwhelming measure, do I want this grace? Do I want it all, or am I only willing to accept a little bit or a minimum, or do I take as much as necessary?

3. *We must bring the Church into this*—Again, this is a Church virtue; it calls for a community dimension. It is not something that exists just for the sake of an individual, but for the sake of the whole community of believers. The way the Church is brought in, the context of this healing experience, is by sharing with the people in my small group just where I am in this whole area of compunction. First of all, have I brought God in? Am I willing to accept that this is a Godly experience, not just a human one? Secondly, where am I as far as desiring compunction? Am I really willing to take it on as it is given to me? I have to be very honest here with my people who surround me.

4. *To see where I have to change in order to accept this grace*—Again, this grace is not in isolation. We have to face the fact that there are some things in my life that definitely are against the possibility of my becoming a person of compunction. Where am I going to attack the pride in my life? Where am I going to increase the humility? What penance do I have to put into my life so I can break down the walls that I have set up? How much more do I have to face into my lack of compassion for the other person in my life?

Once again, the leader is terribly important here. He or she has to be strong with our people, but tenderhearted. He or she cannot allow the strength and the determination that is in him or her to proclaim the Gospel call to compunction, to cause any rough edges in himself or any lack of tenderness in her. On the other hand, that tenderness cannot be an excuse for weakness or failing to offer the fullness of the Gospel message to the people in that group. The point, of course, is not for the leader to provide answers, but simply to provide an occasion whereby the individuals can face into themselves honestly and squarely.

The virtue of compunction can take as much energy and effort (if not more so) than the seeking after compassion. It may well be that an individual or several individuals in the small group may come back week after week. Once again, that should not be a cause of concern, upset, or worry. Certainly such individuals should not consider themselves to be behind or failing. The only thing that would be failing would be to stop coming, either by going on without having accepted the grace or by dropping out completely. The leader has to point this out to them and to explain that staying with this is a good sign, not a bad one. It means we are really being honest with ourselves and furthermore, the grace, once received, will probably stick longer and have more of an impact. The effect on the relationship will also be stronger and more meaningful. Sometimes, as we all know, those quick to accept a grace are quick to lose it. It is the old story Jesus told of the seed that springs up, but it is on shallow soil and there is no place for the roots to sink in.

Humility, Compassion, Compunction—Basically these three virtues call for a tremendous desire and willingness on my part to give up judging. They stop me from standing over somebody in judgment. They take away from me any sense of superiority. They also lead me to a desire to put penance in my life. Penance is an essential dimension to granting forgiveness and accepting healing.

The whole point of this, of course, is not to earn a healing from God. First of all, there is no way we can earn healing. Healing is always gratuitous. Second, God is not like that. We do not have to earn our healing. He offers it freely and spontaneously. The reason we do penance is to purify our hearts so we can accept the healing. That is the real barrier to healing.

Forgiveness—Until I forgive the person who has hurt me, I will not be healed. I do not really want to be healed; I am nursing the hurt and prefer it to the freedom of healing. Were I ever to fully forgive the other person, then I would not have the basis on which to maintain this hurt way of life. No healing can take place without forgiveness. The difference between this kind of healing and emphasis on other kinds of healing in the Church is that here our focus is on relationship. People must be healed and cared for not as individuals in isolation, because they are not. They are taken care of as members of a love relationship and we must never, ever forget that.

Forgiveness is more than calming down and not being angry. It is more than giving up the desire for retaliation and not holding grudges. It is so much deeper than that. *Basically, the forgiveness is in terms of discovering myself, learning that my identity is not me as me. It's me as lover and me as beloved.* Those are not just things I do or accidental parts of my life, or even terribly essential parts of my life. They have changed my identity so that lover and beloved is not a title, nor is it a description of an activity or even of a quality in me. It is me. In a very real sense of the term, I can never define myself or describe myself without describing the other person who is the object of this love relationship and who pours out his or her love on me.

If we have truly been empowered by the Spirit with an overwhelming gift of the three virtues of humility, compassion, and compunction, the forgiveness should naturally follow. Once I have taken my concentration off the mote in the other person's eye and discovered the beam in my own, then I will become ashamed of myself. Then I will have a great compassion for the other person and what they have endured from me. Then I will be humbled. Then my concentration is not going to be on me anymore; it will be on the other person and how I want to restore them to a life of joy and delight. By acquiring these three virtues, we have changed the whole question. Now the anticipation is not what I am going to get out of this experience, it is what my beloved is going to get out of this experience and how I can become a lover again. The fact is, because I have been hurt I have not been much of a lover. Nor have I allowed myself to be a beloved. So we become much more conscious of how we have sinned rather than how we have been sinned against. That is wonderful.

Objections That Might Arise

Of course, there can be objections to this. Suppose the other person is more guilty and has inflicted more pain?

First of all, who is to determine that? There is nobody on the face of this earth who is capable of saying who is the greater sinner or who inflicted the greatest pain. For one thing, everybody's threshold of pain is different. But just by asking the question we indicate that we have not accepted enough of the virtues of compassion and compunction. It is a hopeless question anyway and there is speculation that it is not terribly meaningful and certainly not helpful. The very question itself is like the old question that teenage boys used to ask before going out on a date—"How far can I go with a girl?" Just the very question indicated an improper attitude toward women.

Another difficulty that can arise is we are afraid we will open ourselves to further, even deeper, hurts next time.

Nobody can deny the possibility exists, but all love is a risk. The very fact that I admit to a love is making me vulnerable and putting me in a circumstance where I can be hurt. The only way to avoid the possibility of hurt is to put myself in the greatest hurt of all, which is to cut myself off from any possibility of loving or being loved. The more restrictions I place on my love, the closer I get to that kind of condition. Once again, the reminder is given here that we are talking about fundamentally whole people. We would not ask people to open themselves this way to those who are mentally disturbed or with strong personality defects.

Another problem that arises is, we think it is not fair and it does not seem right that we have to do this.

We have to remember that fairness is not a Gospel quality. That is a bureaucratic quality and an American one at that. It is really a way to avoid responsibility for those we love and who love us and to no longer have to make decisions about them.

But the most important thing we want to face is the hurts that have been deepened by a lack of relationship and loneliness that has been caused by the lack of relationship. The brooding self-pity and the harbored anger has certainly not made my life more cheerful or delightful. I am really not giving up all that much. The price I am asked to pay, if I look at it in itself, may seem very high; but when I look at the present condition I am in and what I am suffering, the price is very low. Furthermore, God takes care of His saints. Once we start walking with God and following His ways, sin loses its power over us and the value systems that sin determines become less attractive. The truth is, sin can only hurt those who are sinners. Sin cannot hurt the saints. This does not mean the saints cannot be physically hurt or that they do not experience rejection. It does mean the power of God's grace is so strong they do not fall into sin in return. That is what the brooding, self-pity, and anger is—sin. That is where the greatest hurts and loneliness of all come in. This is what it really means to say Christ has conquered death. We have been enabled to die to self and to live free in Christ.

7 SUB-GROUP II: IDENTIFYING WHERE I NEED HEALING

This second sub-group should only be entered after the particular virtues of compassion, compunction, humility and forgiveness have been sought and accepted in the first sub-group as confirmed by its members.

It is important to clarify to the participants when entering this process that it is not necessarily the conscious hurt that needs to be healed. Very frequently that is only the symptom, the external circumstance, as in the case of appendicitis. The problem is not the pain in the lower right quadrant of my abdomen, but something deeper. What we are talking about here is the predominant interior attitude such as the following.

A. *Anger*
This is one of the most frequent and devastating of all the symptoms of being hurt. It is not necessarily expressed by loud voices or by stinging remarks. It can be expressed just by challenging or questioning or being suspicious or always looking for the wrong in what the other person is doing or saying. Of course, anger can appear as ice as well as fire.

B. *Self-pity, self-centeredness*
In this regard, one of the things we can do is to examine our conversations and see how often the subject of the

conversation is *me*, or the atmosphere of the home centers around my satisfaction, my mood and well-being.

C. *Independence (Pride)*

This is a very difficult one for us Americans because we are so trained in independence. But basically the way we can recognize it is that we do not like to be identified as belonging to anybody. We become "first name persons"—I am my own man, my own woman.

D. *Consumerism*

We find our identity in our standard of living. Possibly my taste is better than somebody else's so I have fewer things, but those things loom just as large to me as the many things that other people have. It is really a tendency to be middle class.

E. *Desire to be loved rather than to love*

This is a very constant temptation, of course, in which I evaluate my personal relationships in terms of what I am getting out of them, or negatively, how much I am putting into them, and it all seems unfair to me.

F. *Jealousy*

There is a certain mean-spiritedness, a not wanting other people to have what I do not have. This need apply not just in terms of material possessions. It may be expressed in terms of attention or recognition or that somebody in my family seems to be more liked or to receive more attention than I.

G. *Manipulating or controlling others (Power)*

This does not have to be by physical enforcement or even by dominance of personality. Sometimes we can control through weakness, through tears or through making people sorry for us, and so laying guilt on them.

What we could examine is, how happy are people when they are with us and how much do they seem to be jumping to our tune.

H.   Lack of faith in prayer, in scripture, in sacraments
How long have I gone with this hurt and done nothing about it? That really is an expression of despair. I have not turned it over to the Lord; I am trying to handle it on my own terms. Or if I do turn to prayer, it is in terms of changing the other person and getting the other to straighten out or to apologize to me.

I.   Lack of hope, especially in the Resurrection
Just how hopeful a person am I? Am I a person who just lives for the moment, who really is seeing this life as a veil of tears or just living pained?

J.   Lack of reaching out to others
How much of my life centers around me, how much of my focus is what I am getting out of life? Am I giver or a taker? Of course, the people who are the least giving are the ones who always say how little they get, so in their evaluation they are givers. But if people who knew them were asked to identify the most giving people that they knew, would they be at the head of the list?

K.   Desire to be "right"
This is such a curse to all of us. We simply have to prove ourselves to have been correct. Worse, we want other people to salute our flag of being right. How hard do we find it to say, "I'm sorry." Sometimes in families there are members who have never said it in their entire life. Of course, the opposite side of the coin is also true. Sometimes a person says "I'm sorry" but is doing it in order to be right. Very frequently the one who sees self as the peace maker in the family is the one who starts all the wars. Do I always have to be seen as right?

L. *Desire for attention*
When I am in a group of people, especially those who are close to me, is the agenda of the topics of conversation the one I set? Am I the one always talking or are people always addressing themselves to me, or at least are they keeping in the back of their minds, "We have to be careful of what we say or he will get upset or she is not going to be happy, and then we are going to suffer."

M. *Privatism*
This is really a form of apathy, a form of withdrawal. The most obvious experience is the man who goes to sleep on the couch when he comes home from work. That is really a way of getting away, of hiding. But the same thing can be accomplished by a great activism, too, of being tremendously busy. Am I in my own little world and do I only let people in on my terms?

Finding Our Hurt

These symptoms are good clues for us to evaluate ourselves, to recognize that we have been hurt. Because many, many times we kid ourselves; we pretend that we have not been hurt. So we hide behind statements like "I was hurt but I'm over that now." The old saying, "time heals all wounds" is dangerous. Time does not heal anything. At best it dulls our experience of the pain but it does not take away the hurt. Consider the situation where a person has a bad leg and he has gotten so used to walking with a limp that he does not even notice it anymore. But that does not change the fact that the person has a deformed leg. Or we try to kid ourselves and say, "I'm a big boy or a big girl and I've learned to cope with this and into every life some rain must fall."

That is a philosophical position, but not an existential one. Pain is pain; hurt is hurt. The symptoms that are mentioned above are indicative that the hurt is still operative because it is influencing my conduct strongly. One of the best ways for me to recognize that I am hurt is to see how much hurt I am inflicting on others in my life. After all, I am not a bad person or mean-spirited by nature. When I do inflict hurt, it comes more from the pain that I am experiencing than from a direct sinfulness. So we really have to examine ourselves. Sometimes that is not easy. Sometimes in this sub-group what I have to do is to ask my brothers and sisters in the group to help me to identify my hurt. Until I do that, there is going to be no movement forward at all.

But then I have to evaluate if the hurt that first comes to mind is the real hurt, or is there an underlying one? Sometimes a wife, for example, experiences hurt from a husband, but is it really a deepening or a reiteration of a hurt that she experienced from her father growing up? Sometimes, for example, a father experiences hurt from his son, but it really is a living out from another perspective the hurt that he experienced from his father where the father never told him he loved him, and now his son does not. So we have to lead the persons in the sub-group to ask an individual who is describing the hurt to identify when was the first time he or she experienced a hurt like this, not just when was the latest time or the most outstanding time. This can be hard to do, because many times it brings us back to our relationship with our parents and none of us like to face into that. It seems to be disloyal and sometimes it seems to be futile because our parents are in heaven. What we have to recognize is that we can forgive parents who are in heaven and reconcile with them through the power of the Lord.

Writing Down Our Hurt

A very good thing for people who are in this sub-group to do is write what their hurt is. It is important that we give them instructions not to put down a federal case or try to put an indictment down against the person who hurt them.

Very briefly, a format that they could follow is, to just write for a period of time, stream of consciousness style, just putting down hurts that come to mind and going on from there, until they zero in on one major hurt. We can only handle one hurt at a time and should not try to face into a whole bunch of them. So after the stream of consciousness, they come to a particular hurt and in a brief paragraph they describe the event of the hurt—who did it, when, how, where. This should not be long or attempt to condemn the other person and to prove themselves right, but just merely be an identification paragraph. The second paragraph would be a description of how they are presently experiencing that hurt. We are not going into past history now. We are just talking about what is going on inside them. This should be a lengthy and detailed expression of their personal life experience right at this moment, so the other persons in the sub-group can come to true empathy instead of just a knowledge of what went on and what it must feel like. It has to go much deeper than that.

The third paragraph in this writing would be a description of the hurt they are inflicting on others because of the hurt they are experiencing. The purpose of this paragraph is to reestablish and emphasize the compunction that we experience in the previous sub-group, not to justify the hurt that was inflicted on me or to lead me to say, "See, I'm a bigger sinner than the one who hurt me." It is simply to put myself in perspective and to build up within me the power of the virtue of compunction that the Lord is giving to me, so that I can be predisposed to forgive. The compunction is not necessarily directed at the person who hurt me. It is also directed at other people in my life whom I love and whom the Lord has called me to love in return. So, for example, we are not asking a divorced person to reconcile with an ex-spouse and to take up living together; we are not asking a child who as the result of a divorce is in a terrible situation at home and has left to undo the divorce when it is psychologically impossible. We are simply saying that the compunction means to become aware of how many good people in my life who love me are presently being damaged because of the hurt that I am experiencing. This may be taking the format of an active slashing at them or lashing out, but may simply be a withdrawal. Many times men do this in their homes. Because of their hurts, they become quiet and withdrawn and do not expose themselves because they are not willing to take the risk of vulnerability. The compunction is important to get to the stage where I am willing to forgive the person who has hurt me. Until I get to that stage, then I am going to hug the hurt to myself. This is my justification for acting the way I do and until I get filled with compassion, I will not give it up.

Importance of Prayer for Change of Heart

This prayer to change our heart is terribly important. It avoids the whole business of trying to persuade people, to motivate them, or to bring them around by natural arguments. We are simply focusing in on the fact that there is this virtue which this individual member of the

Church needs for the sake of the whole Church and he or she is simply not accepting it. The point is not why or whether it is understandable that they have been hurt so badly; the point is, the Church is being badly limited because of the rejection of the grace. We simply have to call upon the person(s) to change their heart and to accept the power of God's grace to effect that change.

When we started on the healing process, we probably wanted to feel better or to get the strength to cope. That is fine. Whatever got us here to this healing is a good reason. Of course, those motives are perfectly understandable, perfectly human, and grace does build on nature. There is no intention to put those motives down or to say they are bad. We are saying we have to be beyond that by this stage. There has to be a much more essential change of heart than that or the healing will not be real. It will be a facade or a palliative. It is focusing on the activity or the circumstances in my life, not on me and where I need to change. The thrust is not to get the other person to treat me differently, but to get me to treat myself differently. That is the difficulty. I have to stop making myself the center of my life by constantly taking my own temperature, feeling my brow and seeing the condition I am in. I have to start focusing outward and see what I am called to be as a member of the Body of Christ. I need to see that the other people in my life deserve more of me. (Notice the word is "more *of* me" not "more *from* me.") It is not so much the activities in my life which have to change. Probably some of them do; but I myself have to change and that is much deeper.

The healing must come from within. The grace of God empowers us. It is somewhat like in the field of medicine where the body really heals itself, although there is actually no exact parallel because God does the healing. But He does the healing through empowering us to give up what is blocking us from accepting His healing.

Help from the Sub-Group

The whole sub-group has to be praying with the individual person who is seeking the gift of forgiveness. We do not just sit on the sidelines and give advice to the person or persons and tell them that they should forgive. We certainly do not quote scripture at them. Remember that they are good, believing people; otherwise they would not be here. Scripture would come across as an attack. They know that and they will come to it themselves. What we have to do is to pray with them and win from God the power that this person needs, to stand beside them in solidarity before the throne of our Father, to wrestle with God, in order to win an openness in this brother or sister of ours. Of course, forgiveness is to be given not because the person who has offended me deserves it, but simply because the Lord asked me to forgive. Forgiveness is always a gift, never an act of justice. It is not something that I have to do, but something that I offer because the Lord has loved me so much and asked me to forgive as I have been forgiven.

Of course, this has to be a deeply spiritual experience. We have to call upon the cross and mercy of Jesus. We have to allow Him to lead us to a forgiveness that sometimes is beyond our unaided human powers. We have to let the Lord make us more than we could ever be by ourselves. But until the forgiveness is granted, the healing is not going to take place. This is so not because the Lord is punishing us and saying "You're not a good boy or not a nice woman, so I won't do a favor for you," but because we will not accept the healing until we have forgiven. As long as we maintain our unforgiving heart, then we have to keep the hurt in order to justify our lack of forgiveness.

Healing of Memories

Another very important factor regarding the hurts we experience is that frequently they come from the past. Memories are very definitely involved, especially memories of our family relationships over a period of years, especially when we were growing up. Obvious examples of this are people who have a hangup about authority. In many cases, it turns out to be a problem of their relationship with their father which was unresolved. The same thing is true with many angry women.

Once again prayer and scripture has to be dominant here and constant. We cannot just begin the subgroup and then we go onto other things. The Lord first has to be truly present and everyone must be experiencing Him.

What is so tremendously important about memories is that they have an immediately present effect. It is not just that they happened a long time ago in the past and the consequences have continued into the present. The very memory itself is truly present to me right now. That, of course, applies to good memories as well as bad, but in this case, we are talking about destructive memories. Consequently, it is not good enough just to teach people how to cope with the bad effects of things that happen to them in the past. We have to start dealing with the memories themselves because otherwise we are going to teach people an iron-willed capability of overcoming these memories or ways of distracting themselves from them. At best they are temporary and inadequate solutions to the problem.

We have to address the real problem, which is the memory itself. The memory itself has to become a positive memory. We are not implying that we can change the facts, the specific incidents that happened or the relationship that occurred. We are saying we can change our present experience of that memory to a very positive and warm one. So the leader and the rest of the group has to walk the person back through those hurtful memories, back through their life and when they come to a hurtful memory to stop, stay there and really be present to that person in the very experience that created that memory. They have to bring the Lord very dominantly in. No human agency is going to heal this memory. We have to become very conscious as leaders and as members of the little group of our Father's presence right here and now. We have to pour His presence forth upon our brother or sister who we are attempting to provide an occasion for healing. We have to make God so vividly present, so real, warm, gentle, and uplifting that any future coming to mind of that painful memory to the person who is to be healed will be a reminder of His presence to them on that occasion.

Joining Negative and Positive Memories

So now the negative memory is joined by a positive one and the person can choose to emphasize that positive memory. These experiences from here on will remind him or her of Him and how His presence in those very experiences anoint and embrace. The healing of memories is not a magic thing, it is not a wiping out of an eraser. We cannot erase memories as vivid as those which cause present hurt. That just does not happen. We have to bring forth a reality that was existing in that hurtful experience that is also very positive and very true. It is that Jesus was there. We were not conscious or aware of Him.

The point is to bring out the full memory. We are not denying the memory at all. We are trying to fill it out and make it fully real and fully alive so there is no phoniness here, no avoidance of the total experience. The perspective has changed and the reality has changed, but not by taking anything away; rather, by adding something better. That is so much more important and it changes the whole experience.

If a person is having difficulty with advancing toward healing, we simply have to ask them, "Have you forgiven?" This is not done as a challenge, or a put-down, and certainly not asked in any judgmental way, but until they are really struggling with forgiveness and have come to some very true letting go, then the healing process simply cannot take place. That can be particularly hard to do if it is a parent or a spouse or a child who over a period of time has treated me with indifference or has not respected my dignity or has positively damaged me. We have to have a healing of memories here and be led by the Lord to a merciful heart.

Above all, we have to keep reminding the leader of that sub-group that we are not trying to persuade the person to forgive. We have to pray forgiveness into the person; we cannot argue them into it. We are asking of them a forgiveness that is more than a human quality.

Willingness to Accept Healing

Pride is a major obstacle to healing.—We think the one thing we want is to get rid of this pain, but very frequently, we only want to get rid of the pain under very definitive conditions. We do not want to have to admit we are wrong. We do not want to give up our pride. Many times we like the attention we get because of the pain we are suffering and we like being martyrs.

It is hard for us to really come to grips with ourselves. We do not want to face the reality that we are not willing to let go of our pain. It is not that simple. The truth is, we want to get rid of the pain but to do so our way and with very definite conditions. That is what we have to bring to the surface. We have to recognize just what our conditions are, what holds us back from letting go, what weakness in us is at the root of a lot of our pain. It is just like in family relationships, where a child runs away from home. We think he or she is crazy because they have everything at home and their parents are not cruel or inhuman. The boy or girl says they are asking too much of them, or maybe they are too busy for them. Rather than paying the price of getting beyond the defects of his parents, he would rather go through the pain of sleeping on the streets, being lonely and in danger. Divorce, very frequently, is another example. A husband and wife simply will not give in—they are too pride-filled to admit they are wrong and they would rather continue down this adamant line, even though that divorce is inevitable. We do the same thing with our own hurts.

Overcoming Pride
- Penance is terribly important for this sub-group. Pride is a major factor inhibiting us here. The answer to

pride is prayer penance. Through prayer we must try to create a powerful belief in God's love—the whole sense of being held in the palm of His hand.
- Humility is a tremendous need. First of all, we need an acceptance of the Church. It is an essential part of the healing process, to see that healing is not something we accomplish on our own or something just between us and God.

Accepting the Church's Role

Accepting the Church is most important. After all, healing is a charism of the Church. I cannot truly accept God in my life without His people. Otherwise, I accept God made in my image and likeness. I want to bypass that reality; I am focusing completely on my pain. I am not really interested in anything other than if it is going to make me feel better. If I just face into God, then there are no consequences necessarily connected with it. But if I accept the healing from the Church, then my gratitude and responsiveness is going to have to go to the Church rather than just to God, and that is much more threatening. The deep reality is that God has empowered His Church to be the messenger of His healing love. The issue is not whether God can heal or even does heal in other ways. We are saying that the normal way for healing to be experienced in people's lives is through the body of His Son.

When Jesus walked on the face of this earth, He walked as a healer. Did cures take place in other areas? Was sickness of heart or soul healed by Almighty God with people who never were in contact with Jesus? Of course. But, the healing contact with Jesus was much more powerful than just a healing. It offered the Kingdom. The same thing is true with the Church. People are healed in other ways and by other instrumentalities of God than the Church, but the healing with the Church proclaims God's presence in a way that no other healing does, and it brings along the promise of the Kingdom.

One of our problems as healers is that we can get so involved in the suffering the individual experiences and so overwhelmed by the presence of Almighty God that we can tend to ignore the dimension of the Church or perhaps consider it not tremendously important. If so, we are going to deprive people of a great richness that can enter into their lives. We have this richness and we are going to hold it to ourselves unless we are very clear that we have to bring the Church to the foreground. We are going to have to help people to understand that their acceptance of the Church is part of their preparation of heart and soul, and their predisposition for truly allowing healing to take place in their souls.

Healing Is for the Sake of the Church

Much of the reason we hang on to our hurts is because it has become the most important thing about us, the most significant thing in our lives and in the lives of those who know us. We need to get outside ourselves, being willing to be sent by the Church to speak of the love of the Church to others. This is a definite step in healing.

In other words, we are saying that healing is only a beginning. It is not the end in itself; it is a means in God's plan. Too often the person who comes to be healed feels that that is the whole thing. Either they are healed or not healed. Once they are healed, they feel, it is over with. Instead, that is only the start. The healing is never for the exclusive sake of the individual who is healed. The healing is always to proclaim God's presence. Any miracle is a non-verbal prophecy, so anyone who accepts a healing has to be willing to proclaim God's presence in that very acceptance and to continue a life of proclamation of the Gospel. Otherwise, we are just being selfish, concentrating on what we get out of things and very careless about utilizing the power of Almighty God present to us. So we have to be willing to spread the Gospel if we are interested in being healed. God is not just interested in performing wonders and magic tricks. God is interested in letting all people know how much they are loved by Him and how much He wants to enter into their lives. So every contact between God and human beings has that as a purpose, most especially the contact of healing.

A very definite advantage of having an evangelizing mentality and a sense of mission is that it gets us out of our cocoon. It removes the temptation for private relationship with God. It helps us become conscious in a much deeper sense of the term that the purpose of this healing is not just a service performed for me, but a call, a mission, to evangelize.

8 SUB-GROUP III: THE HEALING PROPER

This sub-group is for those who are prepared to accept a healing.

Blessed Sacrament in the Sub-Group

We know the experience of Lourdes, where every day there is a blessing of the sick. Very frequently the cures at Lourdes take place on the occasion of the blessing. It might be a very good idea to strongly consider in the sub-group that directly focuses on healing, that the Blessed Sacrament be taken into that group and that each individual member be blessed with the Blessed Sacrament exposed in the monstrance. It is essential to get away from overemphasis on the human agency of the healing. Just as there can be a tremendous danger of gnosticism, in which we make God a disembodied spirit who works without human agency and apart from the Body of His Son, so too, we can fall into the opposite extreme of making God's part in this most remote, if not invisible. So we can heighten the consciousness of our people that God is in their midst and operating among them. It is God who heals through the use of the Blessed Sacrament and a Benediction, personal and intimate, within that small sub-group.

The Process

A. There must be deep and repeated prayer in this small group for the needs of each member of this sub-group for the particular qualities they are seeking. The participants in this group, having been through three steps in the process, should clearly see the particular barriers they face and are overcoming. Consequently, the focus is very intense.

B. There should be a laying on of hands by each member of the sub-group on the person one at a time.

C. There should be a discernment process as to who should be sent forward from the group of the healers. Definitely the impulse to go to the healers should come from the group rather than from the individual. The small group decides who is ready to move on for more healing.

The Discernment Process

It is just too easy for the individual person to say he or she is ready to go to the healers. That was the whole reason for their coming. Their pain is going to be an impulse for them to seek healing immediately. Therefore, people outside who have a better perspective—the small group that surrounds them and who has been with them, sharing with them and praying with them—can be more honest and open and tell them if they are not prepared to accept a healing. The healing is not going to happen, not because God is not willing for it to happen, but because they are not willing, or because they want a healing that is not real. Any healing that will take place, in their present condition, would only be temporary, shallow, or partial.

The core qualities of a discernment process are first and foremost to experience the presence of the Holy Spirit and to allow the Spirit to guide, direct, and call forth the decision that is made from our hearts. The Spirit has to be at the beginning of the process, not called in to approve a decision we have made for ourselves. All things in this process have to be under His initiative.

The second dimension of a discernment process is that it always has to be for the well-being of the Church as a whole, as the Body of Christ, and not just to respond to an immediate felt need of a particular individual.

The third dimension of a discernment process is, is it going to lead to mission? Is it going to lead to accepting God, first of all, as my Savior and, secondly, as my Lord? Or am I still going to be leading my own life? Very definitely true discernment leads to humility and a giving up, of putting myself in the hands of God.

Whole Sub-Group Accompanies Person

The members of the sub-group surround the person they have decided to send forth to the healers, accompanies him or her, and surround the healers, pouring forth their yearning and their desire for this person to be healed.

This accompaniment on the part of the small group does two important things:

A. *It connects the healing with the process, so that it is not something separate and apart.* That is very important. Once again, it helps to undercut the idea of the healers being dominant and overwhelming. The healers are merely one aspect of the Church reaching out to the hurting person. The members of the sub-group themselves are not just people to be healed, they are part of the healing itself. So immediately we are starting to have a lived out experience of the sense of mission that we mentioned earlier. Every member in that little sub-group thus ceases to be a "problem," but is very definitely part of the solution, a factor in the healing itself. That is a question of reality because none of us are just recipients of the largesse of others. We are also givers. No matter how much we may be in need of receiving, we also are capable of giving. That is important for people not just to know but to experience internally.

We definitely have to help them see how wonderful they are, even in their pain and in the limitations they have placed on themselves because of their pain. Such a going forth with one of the members of their group to the healers shouts out in very clear terms they are not just people to be taken care of, not just a problem. It also has the advantage of reducing the danger of professionalism on the part of the healers, either in fact or in perception, on the part of the healer or of those that are going to the healer. By professionalism we do not mean necessarily something that could seem bad on the surface, but we mean the instances where somebody is convinced that if they do it right, it will take place. By doing right, they mean by focusing on God. But it is them doing it instead of us proclaiming God's presence in our midst and allowing the Lord to operate.

B. *It takes steps to eliminate or at least lessen the danger of one person or one group being thought of as the healers instead of God.* The more we can dispel that notion, the more people we can get involved in the very healing itself, the less danger there is. That is why we have to call on the saints. They are people in the Church. That is why we have the small group accompany the individual and surround the healers and empower the healers by their presence as Church. That is why we should also have the Eucharist exposed.

The healing can take place at any point in the process, especially once compunction has been reached because that is the most important of the spiritual powers that predispose us to accepting the healing presence of the Lord. The process is intended to be a help, not a limitation. Some people will have to go through each of the sub-groups, spending in some cases an extended period of time in one or other of those groups before they accept the particular virtue that is the focus of that sub-group. Others may have such compunction, compassion, or humility that the healing takes place precisely through that experience. In this case approaching the healers is merely to affirm the healing rather than to accomplish it. As Jesus said to the lepers: "Go, show yourselves to the priest."

Note: The purpose of the sub-groups is not to address the hurt but to predispose the person seeking healing to be open to accept the particular spiritual power that is the purpose of that particular sub-group. So each one of those groups is to be dominated by a prayerful environment. It is not what we can do humanly for this person. It is to experience the Lord and to accept His call for us to be full of compunction, forgiveness, or openness to be healed.

No advice or counselling is to take place in sub-groups. People in the sub-group do not address the hurt but the disposition of that person to be healed. The Lord takes care of the hurt. We don't. Our purpose is to share the struggle of the persons and to open their hearts to allowing the Lord to heal them. We are empowering the persons to be healed through our tenderness toward them and sharing our prayerfulness and penitential spirit. The focus in the small group is on the spiritual power that the person must accept from the Lord rather than on how to cope with their hurt, much less take it away from them.

9 WITNESS TO THE HEALING: THANKSGIVING

It is essential to live a life of gratitude. Certainly an increase in the participation in the Eucharist and the Sacrament of Reconciliation should be one of the true fruits of the healing. If such is not the case, then it is very doubtful whether a true, lasting healing has taken place.

Thanksgiving and the Sacraments

When we are talking about an increased participation in the sacraments of Reconciliation and the Eucharist, we are not talking about a payback, but a truly grateful heart in operation. Take the example of a family. When a healing has taken place in a family, the member healed cannot do enough for the other members of the family. It comes out of spontaneous, beautiful, soul-filled generosity, a true response in love. The reason these gifts of the heart are given is because we want to be present to the people who have brought this healing about. We cannot get enough of them.

That is exactly what the Eucharist and Reconciliation are about, being present with our people, the Church, and with the Lord in, with, and through our people. We go to the Eucharist because we cannot get enough of Him and of our unity with one another. The same thing with the Sacrament of Reconciliation and the generosity of soul that leads us to this sacrament. It is not in any way measured. It comes out of a delight. Furthermore, the sacraments must equip me to open myself continuously to God's healing power. As has been experienced in this whole process, it is not always easy to open ourselves. One of the reasons why it has not been easy to open ourselves is that frequently enough our attendance at the sacraments has been sparse. Or even if the frequency is adequate our attendance has been very shallow.

The sacraments bring me more deeply into the Body of Christ. The whole purpose of the sacraments, most specifically Eucharist and Reconciliation, is to draw me into unity with my brothers and sisters in His Body, to empower me to be joined to others as members of the Church. We starve ourselves by our absence from the sacraments.

The best way to express gratitude to the members of the Body of Christ who have created the environment in which I have accepted healing from God is by frequenting the sacraments. Certainly, no one of us who is truly under God's guidance and involved in this healing process would want any reward for ourselves. This is a gift we have been given by and for the sake of the Church. We do not want anything to concentrate on us. What would really please us, though, is if people took on a deeper commitment to the Church, the Body of Christ, and were more willing to be close and intimate with its members, to experience us as a community more fully and meaningfully. That is why the best thing anyone healed can do for us is to take the sacraments on as a way of life rather than just as an intermittent practice.

Leaders Must Set the Example

This frequenting of the sacraments by those healed cannot just be left to happen. With some people that will be evident and they will do it right away. Most people who are healed, however, are coming from much further back as far as the Church is concerned. It is very likely not going to enter into their minds that this is a call to a Eucharistic and reconciling way of life.

So the leadership has to be very active and forthright here. We have to really put ourselves on the line and let the participants know how earnestly we desire this effect among them. Of course, if the Eucharist and Reconciliation does not mean all that much to the leaders, then they are not going to be able to convey this with any sincerity or effectiveness. So the Eucharist and the sacrament of Reconciliation have to be celebrated with vibrancy, enthusiasm, and increasing frequency by those who participate as leaders of one kind or other in this healing process. As the old story goes, we cannot give what we do not have. If we talk about the Eucharist and the sacrament of Reconciliation without enthusiasm, if we are not yearning for these sacraments for ourselves, we are not yearning for them for others. We might recommend the sacramental life as a good idea, but it is not going to be heart-felt and tremendously important to us. We are certainly not going to be able to communicate that conviction.

Core Group

Going to the sacrament of Reconciliation and Eucharist should be a focus of the prayer in the core group, first and foremost for the members of the core group, that they increase in their understanding of eagerness for the sacrament in their own lives and in the lives of those they love. Once again, even if they are going frequently but members of their family are not, it should indicate to them there is something lacking in their own immersion in a sacramental way of life because that should be communicated with their love to their loved ones. Secondly, the core groups should be praying that the Lord grant a passion for the sacraments of Eucharist and Reconciliation among those are participating in the healing process.

It should be talked about a lot before sending the people home. The healer should be talking about it when the people who have been healed and the other sub-groups return to the core group. This should be a topic of conversation. It should be part of the prophecy and the witnessing in the core groups.

Of course, we are not talking about frequenting the sacraments simply in terms of practice. We are talking about them in terms of a way of life and allowing our experience of the sacraments, especially as a sacramental people, to affect our value system and our whole way of living.

Accepting a mission from the Church to bring the love of the Church to others is terribly important in order for healing to be life-giving. Too often the healing is sterile—it is just for the individual involved and how his or her life is now better off. But the Church's life must be better off because someone has been healed. The whole point of any miracle is to proclaim that God is here. And where God is the Church is, not simply an individual. Definitely the complaint of Jesus "Where are the other nine?" has got to be clearly brought out to our people after a healing. They should be coming back to the healing service to praise God in thanksgiving, to win His favors upon the brethren and to open the brethren to accepting the favors that God so generously pours forth.

They should feel a special mission toward others who presently suffer from the same hurts from which they themselves were healed. Certainly this should be the first place they look for a mission. The probability exists that they have something to offer such people, since they themselves have experienced a special sensitivity and responsiveness. Also, they should have a special insight into the areas where blocking can take place among people who experience similar hurts. However, they should not limit their mission and become exclusively involved in one area. There is a danger of professionalism and narrowness fostered by becoming an expert in one area. Ultimately our temptation is to take care of the person ourselves and that does not lead to a healing. At best it leads to someone being taken care of and getting some good ideas on how to cope or how to get out of the hole he or she is in.

Service to All Parishioners

Our people should not consider their mission to be only in circumstances of the healing experience, such as we have just described. A tremendous need exists among parishioners who have not come and maybe never will come to be healed. There is a danger that once somebody has been healed he or she keep coming back to the core group, forming a nice little circle of acquaintances there and never getting outside or beyond it. They should to be part of the prophetic voice that is raised in the core group. We have to ask our people who come to bring this out, how to share God's goodness with others. This means not just by talking about it and giving Him credit for what He has done for us—that is fine and part of the proclamation—but we must also be actively engaged in bringing Him and His Church into the lives of others.

Mission is not a nicey-nice thing where we do some good things for people who elicit our sympathy because they are going through such a tough time. That is normal, humanistic good will. There's nothing wrong with that, but it is just not the charism of healing or a mission of the Church.

Call to Mission

A true healing should call forth a life of gratitude, not simply pulling my share of the load mentally, or a little bit of doing unto others as has been done unto me. I must be much more complete and total in my involvement than that.

Mission must proclaim the Gospel and not stay on the humanistic plane. It must lead people to love the Body of Christ, our brothers and sisters in the Church, not just lead them to a better feeling or set of circumstances in life. If that is all we offer, we are holding back the full richness we have to give. Furthermore, if it is to be a mission, we must accept a sending forth from our brothers and sisters in the parish who have the charism of discernment and who speak for the parish. It cannot be something we do on our own, nor can it be something we are just accountable to ourselves about. There has to be a built-in accountability in our mission.

Healing is also a prophecy and witness to Jesus' presence in our midst. The healing power is essential to the credibility of the Church. The Church of Jesus Christ must be a healing Church. The absence of healing in our midst very definitely casts doubt on the authenticity of the Catholic Church. Every parish, i.e., the community of parishioners including priests and all the people, has a moral responsibility to provide healing. Otherwise we are not serious about caring for our people and proclaiming the glad tidings. One of the greatest glad tidings of all is the possibility of true healing—healing of a person and a love, not just of a body.